The Holy Qur'an
Bears Witness

The Holy Qur'an
Bears Witness

Author:
Mecca LaMacio Medina

WORLD PUBLISHING COMPANY
ARIZONA

The Holy Qur'an Bears Witness Copyright © 2009 Artricia A. Allison. All Rights Reserved. No part of this book may be used or reproduced in any manner whatsoever without written permission except in the case of reprints in the context of reviews. For information, send email to artriciaallison@yahoo.com.

ISBN: 978-0-578-01937-6

Disclaimer: The movements and activities described in this book are solely for educational use. The author and publisher do not intend to present any part of this work as a diagnosis or prescription, nor are they responsible for anyone misrepresenting the material by such claim.

Acknowledgements

As is always the case, there are people to thank. First and foremost I would like to give thanks to Almighty God Allah who appeared in the person of Master Fard Muhammad, to whom praises are due forever, Allah's Messenger Elijah Muhammad, Farrakhan Muhammad, and the whole body of the Nation of Islām the true 5%ers. As a student of the Nation of Islām under the guidance of Minister Farrakhan Muhammad (any mistakes or inaccuracies are mine not Farrakhan's or the Nations); last but not least, I thank Al-Rahīm, the one who love and is merciful, for being present in my life in the person of Malaka Medina AKA Artricia Hunt-Allison, my beautiful and extraordinary wife for her love and support; dedication; insight; mind-set; analysis; and most of all, her friendship. Without her this book could not have been a reality. I thank Allah for such extraordinary woman.

Salām

Mecca Medina

Musaddiq

CONTENTS

WHO OR WHAT IS ALLAH? 10

THE CIRCLE OF GODS 17

WHO IS YOUR MESSENGER? 31

SUNNAH 44

HADITH 54

HADITH EXAMPLES 61

THE DEVIL/JINN 69

SUPERIORITY……..……………………………..90

Preface

I Seek the Assistance of Allah
the Beneficent the Merciful

The reason why I decided to write a book called "The Holy Qur'an Bears Witness" is to get Muslims to take a closer look at their Holy Qur'an. Many Muslims around the world read the Qur'an with a preconceived notion due to over indulging in scholar's interpretation of what the Qur'an says as opposed to reading the Arabic Qur'an for themselves. I'm not saying by no means not to listen to scholars, because it's through persons who study at an advanced level that knowledge and education is passed on from one generation to the next, but what I am saying is that if you are following them (scholars) blindly then that is a problem.

If you are a student of a particular school of thought, you must ask questions and do critical studies. Allah doesn't want us being blind followers. Allah asked of us in the Qur'an—Surah 67:3-4, to look at his creation to see if we can find flaw. Here he is asking us to take on the subject of science. He is asking us to be critical students of his universe. He wants us to study at an advanced level so we will be able to grow into an advanced level of his knowledge, wisdom, and understanding. In other words he wants us to actually know facts of what we are talking about. Allah says in the Qur'an of the Jews, "And some of them are illiterate; they know not the Book, but only hearsay, and they do but Conjecture." (Surah 2:78).

The Jewish masses had no access to their own sacred books, which were known only to their learned men, and therefore religious ideas were based only on stories which they knew from hearsay. Some understand by it the repetition of words without knowing their significance. What is said here about the Jews is to a very large extent true of the Muslims of our day.

In the early days of Islam every individual Muslim man as well as woman sought light directly from the Qur'an. Not so of the Muslims in this age who depend entirely on their scholars. We as Muslims need to get back into the spirit of learning and take time to do a little investigation (in Arabic) to see what the Qur'an actually says for ourselves. No longer should we allow scholars to dictate to us what Allah says when we have the book in our own hands.

Allah says in the Qur'an, "And follow not that of which thou hast no knowledge", (Surah 17:36). Allah wants us to show facts of what we say. The Qur'an tells us concerning unbelievers that when they bring us information ask them to present their proof, as proof is required in order to establish truth. The Qur'an says in Surah 2:111, "And they say: None shall enter the Garden except he who is a Jew, or the Christians. These are their vain desires. Say: Bring your proof if you are truthful." If Allah requires the unbelievers to show proof, don't you think he requires us as believers to show our proof?

The Qur'an tells us in Surah 2:44, "Do you enjoin men to be good and neglect your own souls while you read the Book? Have you then no sense?" We must show facts to what we say. The word "proof" in the English Qur'an is translated from the Arabic word "Burha", which means prove, afford arguments, overcome a person by facts of dexterity. Let us not imitate the ways of the unbelievers; let do as Allah commands us to do - show facts whenever we speak about Allah. Let us be able to show and prove what Allah actually says by way of the Holy Qur'an. I hope you enjoy the reading of this book, and that this body of knowledge can be of help to guide you closer to Allah.

Salâm

WHO OR WHAT IS ALLAH?

As Muslims we hear and use the word Allah on a daily basis probably more than any other word that exist out of all of the languages that is used amongst the human family. But what exactly is Allah? We hear the name we know the attributes, but have no knowledge of it's reality; the actual thing or person and or the name Allah in which these attributes are ascribed to.

If you ask yourself or another Muslim "What is Allah?", the average Muslim will begin reciting attributes such as: Allah is The Aware, The Beneficent, The Helper, etc. Thus, never actually identifying what it "is" that you call Allah or ascribe these attributes to. Exactly what are attributes? The word "Attribute" means; any property, quality, or characteristic that is ascribed to a person or thing. Since Allah has attributes my question is; is Allah a person or thing? The word Allah is a proper noun applied to the Supreme Being. Supreme means; the highest in authority; greatest or most important. "Being" means; existence—whether real or only in the mind.

Question: Is Allah real or does he or it exist only in the mind, abstract—having no material existence?

Before I go any further I want to make sure you, the reader, know what is being asked when asked, "What is Allah?" You must first understand these two words in order to even be in the position to answer this question. The word "what" is an interrogative pronoun used in asking questions related to things, and corresponding in many respects to who, what person, or persons. The word "is", is the 3rd person singular of the verb to "be". "Is", is one of the six forms of "be" showing the present tense, to have a real state of existence; to exist in the world of fact. So, is Allah *real*, or is Allah a *thing* that is inferior to man?

Let's stop asking questions and go to the Holy Qur'an and see what it says of Allah.

In the Qur'an, Allah is referred to as "Alla<u>dh</u>î" which means; he; the man who. The conjunctive "Al-la<u>dh</u>i" is compounded of the article "Al" the demonstrative letter "lam" and the demonstrative pronoun "<u>dh</u>ā" or "<u>dh</u>ū". When used substantively it has the same meaning as "man", "mā", viz, he (the man) who, which, that, and whatever; when used adjectively, it agrees like any other adjective, with its antecedent, which is always a definite (serving to designate a person or thing that is or can be immediately identified) substantive (substantial; having substance: material, not imaginary: real) with which it agrees in gender, number and case." That's why scholars like to translate the word Alla<u>dh</u>î to "who". The word "who" means; what or which person or people; introducing more information about someone just mentioned.

The Qur'an Sura 7:54 says in part: "INNA - Rabba - Kumu - Allah - Alla<u>dh</u>î"

Translation: "....Surely your Lord." ".....is Allah who (person)"

The Qur'an Sura 13:2 says in part: "Allah - Alla<u>dh</u>î"

Translation: "Allah is he who (person)"

The word "Alladhi" clearly shows that the Qur'an is speaking of Allah as a person; and to prove that this word is used and means "person" the Qur'an uses the same word "Alladhî" in its plural form in Sura 18:28; "Was - bir - nafsaka - ma'al - ladhîna"

Translation: "And keep thyself with those (persons)

Now, let us take a look at the word "Ahad". This word means one man; someone; somebody; anyone. Some scholars say that this word is applied to Allah alone, and that the word "Ahad' means one as in - the cardinal number; one, single. But that can't be further from the truth, as I said the word Ahad means: someone, somebody, anybody. And the word "Ahad" is not just applied to Allah alone.

The Qur'an Sura 72:2 says in part: "Wa - Lan - Nushrika - bi - rab - bi - nā - Ahad"

Translation: "And not associate with our Lord anyone."

As you can see the word anyone is a translation from the Arabic word "Ahad", which is not used in referring to Allah. Let us look at these Suras below:

The Qur'an Sura 72:26 says: "Alimu - AL - Ghaib - falā- yuzhiru-álâ Ghaib-bi-hi-Ahad"

Translation: "Knower of the unseen, so he makes his secrets known to none"

The Qur'an Sura 72:7 says: "Wa - anna - hum - Zannū - Kama - Zanan - Tum - anl - lan - yabath - Allah - Ahad"

Translation: "And they thought, as you think, that Allah would not raise anyone"

As you can see the words; "anyone" in 72:7 and "none" in 72:26, are both translations from the Arabic word "Ahad". "Ahad" is a masculine singular noun, meaning; person, anyone. Even "Abdul Mannân" Omar, in his dictionary of the Holy Qur'an says on page 12, "Ahad signifies oneness of God in his person." These verses clearly show that this word "Ahad" is referred to a person. Now let us examine Sura 112, because this is one of the Suras that some Muslims use to argue that Allah can't be a man because none is like him. Let's see what the Qur'an has to say……

The Qur'an Sura 112:1 says: "Qul - huwa - Allah - Ahad"

Translation: "Say: he, Allah is one"

Question: One what? One as in the Cardinal Number: one, single. That's not true because the Qur'an would have used the word "Wâhid" as the Qur'an does when referring to Allah as singular or alone. But the word "one" here in Sura 112 is translated from the Arabic word "Ahad" meaning; one man (person). "Say; he Allah is one man." That would be the correct translation.

The Qur'an Sura 112:2 says: "Allah– AL - Samad"

Translation: "Allah the Eternal"

The word "Samad" actually means more than just eternal. It actually means; The Supreme being who is independent and be sought of all and unique in all his attributes. Showing us that Allah is a person that is not equal to any other; this person (Allah) is unique. Lets just see how unique the person is in verse (3).

The Qur'an Sura 112:3 says: "Lam - yalid - wa - Lam - yûLad""

Translation: "He begets not, nor is he begotten".

A lot of Muslims believe that this verse proves that Allah is not a man (person), but that is not true at all - all this verse says is that he *begets* not.

Now in order for a man to reproduce (father a child), he needs a mate (woman) that is if you are going according to the law of nature. I know a lot of you think that the law of nature doesn't apply to Allah, but in fact it does. Remember the Christens attributed sons and daughters to Allah, but to prove them wrong in the Qur'an Sura 6:101 asked "How could he (Allah) have a son when he has no consort?" The word "consort" is taken from the Arabic word "Sâhibat" meaning; spouse; wife. Now we know it's impossible for man to reproduce without a woman, right? But here we have the Qur'an telling us, through the form of a question, that it's impossible even for Allah to produce a child out side of the law of nature. So, if the laws of nature doesn't apply to Allah, then why would Allah use them as an argument to show that he didn't have a son? Think about it!

The Qur'an said: "Nor is he begotten". Allah is not begotten because he is the first. The "essence" of himself existed before the physical, Allah is "Quyyûm"; self existing. Allah created himself (the physical) out of the material of darkness. Before there was anything there was darkness, but it was a substantive darkness. But matter was in the darkness, even though matter was in the darkness it is considered nothing, because it was without aim and purpose. Anything without aim and purpose is considered nothing. But the "light" in that darkness was electricity, the energy which is Allah himself.

The first two words in Sura 24:35 are "Allah Nur" meaning Allah is light. "Nur" is that form of radiant energy, the source that manifested and produced everything that exist. It produced the first germ of life. The first atom of life sparked in the darkness. There was no physical at that time just energy. Nothing was acting by way of thought. Thought is just a word that describes energy in relation to the brain vibrating at a very high frequency. There was no brain at that time so there forth there was no thoughts, everything was automatic acting by the will of Allah.

Once the physical part of the universe came then Allah produced his person. The word person comes from the Latin word personare; Per means through and sonare means to sound. The word "person" is nothing more than a bodily form, the frame that is used to contain the spirit (energy). Once energy is contained within the brain only then can man be produced. The word man comes from the Latin word "mens", which means "mind". Where there is no mind there is no man. So now we understand why verse (4) says: "Wa-Lam-yukûnl-Lahu-Kufûan-Ahad".

Translation: "and none is like him."

Now, that is the translation you will find in most of your Qur'ans. I am going to give you a word for word translation. "Wa-Lam-yukûnl-Lahu-Kufûan-Ahad"

Translation word for word: "and not exist with him equal one man"

Showing us that none that exist is equal with this one man. The word "like" was taken from the Arabic word "Kufuwan" which means, equal. So, the Qur'an here is not telling us that we're not like Allah, because the word "like" means; a person or thing that's similar to another; meaning similar but not identical. To hold the view that no one is like Allah is inconsistent with the whole of the Qur'an, and that goes for Sura 42:11 as well, that use the word "Kamith".

Sura 42:11 says: "The originator of the heavens and the earth. He has made for you pairs from among yourselves, and pairs of the cattle, too, multiplying you thereby. Nothing is like him; and his the hearing, the seeing." The phrase "nothing is like him" reads in Arabic, "Laŷsa– Kamithilihi - Shaiun", the Arabic, "Mithl" means; likeness; like; similar; equivalent; equal.

The combination of "Ka" is use to put emphasis on the word "Mithl". Showing that none is "Equal" to Allah on no level. To translate the word "Mithl" to like, meaning; similar or similarly, would contradict the whole of the Holy Qur'an. Sura 16:60 clearly tells us that the highest similitiude belong to Allah.

Sura 16:60 reads in part: "Wa-Lillahil-Mathalul-A'lâ". Translation: "And belong to him (Allah) is the highest similitude." And Sura 30:27 repeats the same thing. The Qur'an is not saying here that none isn't like or similar to Allah, but rather showing how no one is his equal. Sura 41:9, "Say: Do you indeed disbelieve in him who created the earth in two days, and do you set up equals with him?" This is where the unbelievers went wrong, they always tried to set up equals with Allah, but there is none equal to Allah. And the unbelievers realized this as time went on.

Sura 26:97-99 says, "By Allah! We were certainly in manifest error, when we made you equal with the Lord of the worlds, and none but the guilty led us astray." None is equal to Allah the first, but we are all like him. The Qur'an clearly tells us in Sura 7:151 that Allah is the most merciful of those who show mercy. Most merciful was taken from the Arabic word "Arham" and those who show mercy is taken from its plu. "Râhimîn", which clearly shows that Allah is not the only one who shows mercy; that it is others who shows mercy as well. Showing that we have similar characteristics, but Allah is the best. And none is equal to him. (Sura 19:65) But we are all "like" him, Allah is the creator and we are creators as well.

In Sura 37:125 Elias asked the question: "Do you call upon Ba'l and forsake the best of the <u>creators</u>?" The Arabic word for creators is "Khâliqîn", which means: creators; those who determine. "Khâliqîn", is the plural of "Khalq", which means: the measuring out or resolving of the thing out of pre-existing matter. Isn't that what we do as human beings?

Look at the world around us; cars, homes, clothes - everything was created from pre-existing matter, and who created them - We did! But Allah created the sun and the entire universe in which we live. So now you can see how we are all like Allah, but we can never be equal to the first. The Most Honorable Elijah Muhammad said we are all Allah! Now how can we all be Allah when Allah is one? And we just learned that we can't even be his equal, but now The Honorable Elijah Muhammad is telling us that we are all Allah. Sounds like a contradiction doesn't it?

Let's see...in Sura 4:1 the Qur'an tells us that Allah created us from a single being. The word "being" is taken from the Arabic word "Nafas", meaning; mind, spirit; person. The Qur'an also tells us that after Allah created us he placed himself in us.

Sura 15:29 says: "So when I have made him complete and breathed into him of my spirit, fall down making obeisance to him."

The word "spirit" is taken from the Arabic word "Ruh", which means; essence. Essence are the qualities or element making something (or person) what it is. So, what Allah (the first) did here was shared himself with many. Share means to divide. If Allah is "one" and divided himself with (let's say) 200 people; one goes into 200 0.005 times. So that means that each person would have 0.005 percent of Allah within them - Right?

Now, if those 200 people were to unite - 0.005 x 200, what you would have is one essence; but plural only in persons. Those who are used for the "one" to sound through. That's why we as Muslims believe in the unity of Allah. Unity is many parts coming together as a complex whole. Allah is a word that comprises all the attributes of purification. Instead of reciting hundreds upon hundreds of attributes, we sum them up with one word - Allah. When we are told in the Qur'an to serve Allah we are actually being told to become Allah. To become that which is in us.

Sura 11:2 - "That you should serve none but Allah. Surely I am to you from him a warner and a giver of good news."

The word "serve" is taken from the Arabic word "Ta'budu", which is another form of "Ibâdat". The impress of divine attributes and imbibing and reflecting them on ones own person. The ideal of "Ibâdat" in the Qur'an lies not in a mere declaration of glory of Allah by lips and performance of certain rights of service (i.e.

prayer, fasting, etc.) but it is in fact the imbibing of divine morals and receiving the impress and imbibing of these attributes.

It is only when we submit our will to Allah's will (the first), that we can be excepted in the circle of Gods and become one with Allah. There is only one God, the word "God" only takes on the plural form due to the many different persons that Allah use to transmit his essence through. So there are many Gods in person, but one in essence (mind). With there being only one mind, there is only one determination, aim, purpose and goal; and that is to do the "Will of Allah". That's why the Qur'an tells us in Sura 23:91; that if there were more than one God ("ilah", meaning; someone worthy of worship) - each would try to take away what they created. But Allah is one (of one mind) on one accord. So when, The Honorable Elijah Muhammad said that we were all Allah, he was taking us beyond the physical straight to the essence of who we really are.

Sura 31:30 tells us that Allah is the only reality. So if Allah is the only reality, then what are we? Do we really exist? The Arabic word is "AL-hagga". "AL" is the definite article, it is equivalent to "the" in English. In Arabic it is used to give the meaning of; most, all, complete, maximum, whole and to denote comprehensiveness. "Hagga", meaning reality. So not only is Allah the whole reality, but he is a comprehensive reality. So if you exit (and you do), then that means that you are a part of Allah and Allah is apart of you, which means that you are a part of that one reality.

When we think of ourselves as a separate reality outside of Allah we disconnect ourselves from Allah all together. Sura 7:157 commands us to follow that which is good. The word "Ma'rûf", meaning that which is good as in a universal accepted fact, opposite to "munkar", which means; what is strange to the human nature. Allah wants us to follow that which is in accordance with facts; to accept anything other than that would be to deny the reality of Allah himself.

The ten-percent and the eighty-five percenters try to make us, five-percenters, believe that Allah can't be comprehended. But the Qur'an tells us that Allah is "AL-Hagga", a comprehensive reality. If Allah is something we can't comprehend then that means Allah is something we have no knowledge of. The Qur'an orders us in Sura 17:36 not to follow that of which we have know knowledge. Allah can be comprehended and must be understood within the realm of reality.

What was Abraham's idea of Allah, was Abraham's idea within the realm of reality? He accused his people of worshipping things that couldn't eat, hear, see, speak nor benefit or harm. So that means that Abraham's God was opposite of that in which he accused them of worshipping - Right? So how did his God carry out the function of eating, hearing, seeing and speaking without the physical organs that is needed in order for these senses or actions to work?

In order for you to hear you first need the organ of hearing; which in man and higher animals is composed of the external ear, a cartilaginous funnel for collecting the sound waves and directing them inward; the middle ear, tymyanum or drum; and the internal ear or labyrinth; creating the sense of hearing allowing us to perceive sound; that which is heard; the effect which is produced by the vibrations of a body affecting the ear. The Qur'an bears witness that these physical organs are needed.

Sura 7:195 - "Have they "feet" with which they walk, or have they "hands" with which they hold, or have they "eyes" with which they see, or have they "ears", with which they hear?"

Sura 37:91-92 - Abraham's God must of eaten food as well, because he turned to their Gods and said "Do you not eat? What is the matter with you that you speak not".

All of this was said to show that Abraham thought of his God not as a mystery or spook, but as a real live human being different from you and I only in that he is supreme in knowledge, wisdom, understanding and power. But, it wasn't the physical that Abraham worshipped, it was that in which the physical contained. The physical is a veil that covers the essence of the person. We don't worship the physical. Allah is "ever-living" who never dies. The flesh is finite so the flesh is not the God, it's only the house of God. Allah is the supreme power of the universe, that in which the physical contain. Now that we have a realistic understanding of Allah, let's see if we can understand something about his physical origin.

Sura 57:3 says: "He is the first and the last and the manifest and the hidden and he is the knower of all things."

The word first is taken from the Arabic word, "Awwal", which is the singular (n.m.) form of the plural form "Awwalûn" or "Awwalin" (found in 15:13), meaning; Ancients; those of former days. Awwal comes from the root word "Âl", meaning; family, race, dynasty, people. So basically what the Qur'an is telling us here is that Allah is of the first race of people that exist on earth; showing that the original people contained Allah (the supreme mind) within their persons, which made them a dynasty people, because the supreme knowledge, wisdom, understanding and power is pasted on from one to another. Making sure the supreme wisdom is always kept within the family (which we'll get into later). The word "last" is taken from the Arabic word "Akhiru" meaning; last; that is to come; later; after. Showing us that Allah will come to do his work after the works of Satan. Allah allows Satan a period of time to work.

Sura 15:38: "Till the period of the time made know".

The time made known is the time when Allah manifest himself. The word "manifest" comes from the Arabic word "Zâhir", which means to appear, become distinct, come out. Why would Allah have to appear, become distinct or come out? Was he hidden? Yes! Sura 2:2-3 tells us that those who keep their duty are those who believe in the unseen. The word unseen comes from the Arabic word "Ghaib" - hidden reality. Where was this reality hidden and why?

Allah became hidden because the original man lost his true identity of self (except the circle) – we'll get into that later as well. In Sura 57:3 the word "hidden" comes from the Arabic word "Bâtin", which means; hidden; inner-part; inside; interior. Showing that Allah was hidden within the inner-part of man and will remain hidden until man get a true knowledge of self. That's why Satan said in Sura 15:36 - "My Lord, respite me till the time when they are raised". Because it is only when we get knowledge of self that we can bring an end to the devils rule and place ourselves in the position in which we were created to be; the rulers of the universe. The only way we can get back to that state of mind, we have to be educated with God knowledge. The Qur'an said that Allah is the knower of all things. But how did Allah come to know all things?

Sura 6:80 Abraham said: "My Lord comprehends all things in his knowledge".

Arabic: "Wasiá - rabbi - Kulla - Shaîin - Ilm".

Translation word for word: "comprehend - Learned in divine law - All - things - science".

So the Qur'an is telling us that Allah is learned in divine law and comprehends all things through knowledge. But what kind of knowledge? The word knowledge is taken from the Arabic word "Ilm". In Arabic there are two words translated to the English word knowledge. "Arafa" and "Ilm" the difference is:

"Arafa" is a fact and knowledge that is specific but yet more general; whereas the word "Ilm" is a distinct and specific knowledge; a supreme science. The Qur'an is showing us that it is only through supreme knowledge that we can become masters of self and the universe. We must stop looking outside of ourselves for a mystery God, and start looking for the God within us. It's only through knowledge of self that Allah can be made manifest and bring an end to the devils rule. Now back to our original question: *Who or what is Allah?*

Answer:

(1) Allah is Al-nur, that form of radiant energy that produced everything that exist. That in which nothing could exist without, that which is non-local ever enduring, kinetic energy causing life, chemical energy undergoing a change of composition decaying causing death.

Allah is also a word that comprises all the excellence attributes of good; merciful, compassionate, etc.

Allah is Al-A'lâ; the most high, the name that is used to represent Al-mala (n.plu.); the Chiefs (the circle of Gods) - which will be explained later.

Allah is the proper noun applied to the supreme being. The only person who can wear Allah as a personal name is the supreme one amongst the circle—M. F. Muhammad.

Salâm

THE CIRCLE OF GODS

Understand that the word Allah is neither singular or plural, masculine or feminine. Allah is a word that represent a unit. A unit is a noun, an individual thing, person or group that's a part of a complex whole. Now, in the Qur'an Sura 5:48 it says; "And we have revealed to thee the Book with the truth...." in Arabic the words "we have revealed" are "Wa-anazal-na". The Arabic word "Anzal" means to send down. But what is intrusting is what's connected to the end of the word "Anzal", is the Arabic word "Na". "Na" is a pronoun plural meaning "we".

We is a word that is used when someone is referring to themselves and others. We is also frequently used by individuals, as editors, authors, and the like, when alluding to themselves in order to avoid the appearance of egotism; the plural style is also used by Kings and otherwise heads of countries, which is called the royal we.

Scholars like to make us believe that when the Qur'an use "we" and "us" it is using the royal we as if Allah need to avoid the appearance of egotism. Let's allow the Holy Qur'an to speak for its self and see which usage best fits the context. One of Allah's attributes are "Al-A'lâ", which means "The most high" and this word is used in its elative form showing that it is the highest the acme, nothing is greater than it.

Keeping that in mind let's go through Sura 37:1-4:

    1. "By those ranging in ranks."

    2. "And those who restrain holding."

3. "And those who recite the reminder."

4. "Surely your God is one."

Let's take a closer look at verse four (4). The Arabic word used for God is "Ilah" not Allah. Why? The word Allah holds a much greater significance than the Arabic word "Ilah". "Ilah", means to adore, worship, deify any one, call anyone worthy of worship. It even has its plural and dual forms. "Ilâhain" (dual) two Gods, "Âliha" (n. plural) Gods. My question is, why would the supreme use a word for himself, that was used for idols? It's because no where in the Qur'an did Allah deny the existence of other Gods (Âliha). Allah tells us in Sura 17:22, "Associate not any other God (ilah) with Allah." How could Allah tell us not to associate other Gods with him if no other Gods existed? The very statement itself bear's witness to their existence.

The word "Associate" in 17:22, comes from the Arabic word "Ja'ala" which means; esteem or regard. Sura 17:22, is telling us not to hold any other gods in the same regard or esteem as Allah. But, you have to understand that we are all lesser gods, and to refer to ones self as a god isn't wrong or a sin. The Qur'an tells us in Sura 21:29, "And whoever of them should say, I'm a god besides him, such a one we recompense with hell." The word "besides" is taken from the Arabic word "Dûna", which means; inferior or superior; more important. To render the word "Dûna" to the english word "besides" is misleading. What Sura 21:29, is telling us here, is that, if anyone should say he is a god superior; meaning higher in authority or rank, such a one Allah (The Supreme) will recompense with hell. Allah never denied the existence of other gods, he denied the doctrine of the unbelievers who taught that other gods were equal to or superior than Allah himself. Sura 17:42, says; "Say: if there were with him (Allah) gods, as they say, then certainly they would have been able to seek a way to the Lord of the Throne." "The phrase "Kamā-Yaqūlūn" meaning "as they say" clearly shows us that Allah denied the doctrine of the unbelievers not the fact that other gods exist. Understand that the word Allah is also a proper noun, a name, that is worn by the Supreme Ilah (God) to distinguish himself from others.

Sura 4:171 in part it says: "inna-mal-lahu-ilahunw-wahid."

Translation: "only Allah God is one."

Notice here in this particular verse that the word "Ilah" is preceded by the word Allah. Showing us that the word Allah is used as a proper noun here worn by the Supreme Ilah (God). That's why it says in Sura 112:1, "Say he Allah is one." Ahad is a noun that is used in it's substantive from showing that this man (Ahad) is self existent, having a real existence; actual; of or containing the essential elements. This is not an imaginary man, he is real. But this man doesn't act alone he has associates.

Now how can I make such statement after reading Sura 6:163, which says: "No associate has he". Its because I'm not lost in translation. The word associate here is taken from the Arabic word "Sharîka" meaning one who shares. Sura 17:111 reads: "And say: Praise be to Allah who has not taken to himself a son, and who has not a partner in the Kingdom..."

Partner in the Kingdom in Arabic is "Sharîkun-fil-mulk". Sharîka means; Polytheism; Idolatry; making associate or partner (in worship) with Allah. "Fi" means - in, and "Mulk" means, dominion, one who possesses power. So what the Qur'an is telling us is that, we are not to associate (in worship) any other God with Allah, because it's Allah and Allah alone that has supreme power." That's why in Sura 7:54 it says, "and he is established on the throne of power."

The phrase "Throne of Power" is taken from the Arabic word "'Arsh", which literally means a thing constructed for shade or anything roofed; but the word is used as a metaphor in the Qur'an meaning power and control. The only way one can have power or control of the universe, one must have supreme knowledge. So what the Qur'an is showing us here is that Allah has supreme knowledge.

Sura 2:255 in part; "His throne extends over the heavens and earth..." The Arabic word is "Kursi", which means knowledge showing that Allah's knowledge is above all (Sura 12:76). So Allah is not saying he doesn't have helpers, he is only saying that none has equal knowledge to the one supreme. That is why Sura 17:111 goes on to say; "And who has not a helper because of weakness." The word helper is taken from the Arabic word "walî" meaning, helper; friend and successor, showing that Allah does have associates, but eliminating any misconception in thinking that Allah has associates due to being weak.

Now lets go back to Sura 5:48 - "And we have revealed to thee the book with the truth." So who is this we? They are the exalted chiefs; the associates and helpers of Allah (the supreme Ilah). They act from the mind of the one supreme. They contain the knowledge of the mysteries of the universe. That is why soothsayers and devils are always trying to tap into the supreme knowledge of the "Al-Mala', Al-A'lâ" meaning; the most high, chief men, assembly. (Sura 15:18); but the Qur'an tells us in Sura 37:7-8, They cannot listen to the exalted assembly."

The word exalted is taken from the Arabic word "Al-A'lâ", which is an attribute of Allah meaning '"the most high." The word assembly is taken from the n. plural, "Al-mal'a" meaning, the chiefs men, the leaders, the heads, the assembly. The word assembly is a noun meaning an organized group of persons. And it is this circle of men that is referred to by the Qur'an as "the most high" (elative). This shows and prove that the word Allah is also used for the Circle of Gods as well as a personal name that is worn by the supreme one from amongst the circle.

Now "we" can understand why the Qur'an use the plural we when referring to delivering the revelation.

The Honorable Elijah Muhammad taught us that there are twenty-four (24) wise men who do the work of producing the Bible and Qur'an. He said they make history (Bible and Qur'an) to equal the circumference of our home (earth); one year for each mile. So the book that is written contains twenty-five thousand (25000) years of history written in advance. And when the time comes for a certain part of the writing to be fulfilled, one of the wise men (Al-malā'a Al-'Alâ) will speak to someone amongst the people to reveal a part of the writing (scripture), and give him an assignment or mission.

The Honorable Elijah Muhammad said that he who rules that cycle of history is called the supreme being and wears the name Allah for himself. The Holy Qur'an tells us that revelations has a particular time to be revealed. Sura 6:67 says; "for every prophecy is a term, and you will soon come to know"; which shows that the knowledge of the revelation (prophecy) is already known with Allah (The Circle), but will be revealed to the people at a particular time. This bear's witness that it was already determined (written) in advance. Sura 57:22, "No disaster befalls in the earth or in yourselves, but it is in a book before we bring it into existence - surely that is easy to Allah."

Prophet Muhammad was chosen to receive the Holy Qur'an - Sura 38:69-70 quotes Muhammad; "I have no knowledge of the exalted Chiefs when they contend." "Only this is revealed to me that I am a plain warner." Showing that the one who revealed the message to him was one of the exalted

Chiefs, and came to him under the name Gabriel (Arabic—Jabrîl) (Sura 2:97). Jabrîl is a compound word made up of the Hebrew Jabr (person) and îl (God) meaning, God in person, or person of God. In Arabic Jabar is the root word for the Arabic word Jabbâr, which is an attribute of Allah used in Sura 59:23. So understand that Gabriel is not one individual, but a title worn by different men at different times in history delivering the message to a particular chosen one.

Now the Qur'an teaches us that Allah is the creator of the earth. But in Sura 15:23, it says; "And surely it is we who give life and cause death, and we are the inheritors." Now we all know that Allah is the one who gives life and cause death, but once again Allah here is represented by the plural "we". Then the verse goes on to say, "we are the inheritors." Now wait a minute! The word inheritors is taken from the Arabic word "Wârithūn", which means to inherit or become owner or sustainer of somebody or thing after someone; succeed, take the place previously filled by; come next in order.

Who came before Allah? And what is Allah the inheritor of? Sura 19:40 says; "Surely we inherit the earth and those thereon". So not only did Allah become owner of the earth, but he was given power over all that's on earth. Now how did this happen? And who gave Allah power? These are some intelligent questions. But understand that no one gave Allah power. The word Allah here is used to represent the Circle and the Supreme One of the Circle at the same time. Before the physical the power of Allah (The Supreme) existed alone within the darkness of the universe as potential energy, that which has the ability to work. Once the power became kinetic, causing the first motion slowing down its vibration densing itself to bring about that which we refer to as matter, that which has weight and take up space. Then the atom went through a chemical change, a process in which the properties of substance change and new substance formed producing new kinds of matter.

The essence of matter is energy, which is "Rabb", that which fosters and brings up and regulate the things from the crudest state to that of the highest perfection; in such a manner as to make it attain one condition after another until it reaches its goal of completion, which in the physical world is the human form. But the human form isn't perfect, but it's the best conveyor for the power of Allah (mind).

Once the first person (the supreme mind in its physical) mastered himself, he willed into existence others of his kind (physical beings) by "be and it is". And then he set up the law of life and death, with a supreme knowledge kept amongst a selective few on how to escape death. Allah knew that the physical body that was made for himself and others was finite and that it wouldn't last forever. The body goes back to the earth, but Allah (power, mind) never dies. There is always a physical form (person) coming up that will allow him to transmit his knowledge, wisdom and power through that physical form. The person who receives that wisdom becomes the inheritor of the earth, power, and knowledge over all things on earth; the same one and only God, but a different form. This is how Allah gives power to himself and inherits the earth. With this process continuing the supreme knowledge always stays within the Circle of Gods, allowing the supreme to continue to live forever. That is why he is the ever-living who never dies.

Now is it possible for us to escape death and live forever? If so, how? First, we must master self and bring out the God from within. Allah is that supreme power in us all. It is the essence of who we are, so we are all Allah in essence. But when we lost knowledge of self the light (supreme mind) within went out. Now we need someone from the original power source to reactivate conscious awareness of self. And only then will we be accepted back into the Circle of Gods and can live up under the name Allah and liver forever.

Sura 55:26 says: "Everyone on it (earth) will pass away".

Sura 16:96 says: "What is with Allah will endure"

So who is the one from the original power source who can reconnect us back with Allah (Phonetics; All-Law)? Well let's see! The Holy Qur'an tells us in Sura 3:7, that some of its verses are decisive and some are allegorical, and that none know the allegorical verses but Allah. So did Muhammad know? Because if not (which he didn't) that means Muhammad was only able to teach the Muslims of his time the basics of the Qur'an. Because the only parts of the Qur'an he would have understood were the verses that are decisive. The word decisive is taken from the Arabic word "MuhKamât", which means clear, and is to be taken in its literal sense.

Now lets look in the Qur'an and see exactly how much knowledge Muhammad had of the Holy Qur'an. Sura 17:85 quotes Muhammad, "And they ask thee about the revelation. Say: The revelation is by the commandment of my Lord and of knowledge you are given but a little." The word rūh; meaning inspiration or revelation refers to the Holy Qur'an itself, Sura 42:52 also bears witness to this fact.

Before this verse as well as after it, the Qur'an is the only topic of discussion, and therefore the context shows clearly that the question is not about the soul of man, for which the proper word is "nafs", but about the Qur'an itself. They were given little knowledge of the Qur'an because Muhammad only knew the decisive verses there of. Whenever someone has knowledge or information that is only known to ones self, it is called a secret. The knowledge of the allegorical verses is one of Allah's secrets. And another one of his secrets is the knowledge of the day of judgment. But the Qur'an tells us that Allah's secrets will be made known to a messenger whom he choose. Muhammad of fourteen hundred (1400) years ago was "not" that messenger.

Sura 72:25-27 quotes Muhammad, "Say: I know not whether that which you are promised is nigh or if my Lord will appoint for it a distant term." "The knower of the unseen, so he makes his secrets known to none." "Except a messenger whom he chooses."

So the messenger Allah choose to reveal his secrets to would be the one who would know the meanings to the allegorical verses. Right? So that's why the Qur'an tells us in Sura 11:1, "I, Allah am the seer. A book whose verses are characterized by wisdom, then they are made plain from one wise, aware."

Now who is this one, this messenger who Allah chose to give such secrets to? The one who possess the secrets of Allah has to be one who possess supreme knowledge; because he is the one who is going to make the Qur'an plain. The word "plain" is taken from the Arabic word "fussilat", which means to expatiate into detail, to teach the book with all its particulars.

Who is this one? Notice the words "Hakîm" and "Kabîr" in Sura 11:1 doesn't have the definite article "Al" (the) attached. Showing that this verse is not referring to the supreme Allah himself, but to someone who is wise, aware. These attributes are telling us something of the person here. The word "wise" is taken from the Arabic word "Hakîm" meaning one who possess quality which discriminates between truth and falsehood and is free from incognity or doubt. The word "Farrakhan" comes from the Arabic word "furqân" , which is one who distinguish between truth and falsehood.. Sounds a lot like Hakîm?

The messenger who was sent to the Asiatics in the wilderness of North America was the Honorable Elijah

Muhammad. He was the messenger who Allah chose to reveal his secrets to, but he was not the one who would explain the Qur'an in detail. Elijah Muhammad only taught 2/3 of the Qur'an while he was in our presence.

The Qur'an says in Sura 44:5-6, "That out of his (Allah) mercy messengers are forever being sent." The Qur'an also tells us that a witness will be raised out of every people from amongst themselves, and we all (those who have knowledge of self) bear witness that we have a witness in our presence today; but what we don't understand is that the witness is a messenger as well.

Sura 73:15 "Surely we have sent to you a messenger a witness against you, as we sent a messenger to Pharaoh." This witness was sent to carry out a particular role as Aaron was sent to carry out a particular role for Moses.

Even though Aaron was sent to be the helper of Moses, he took on the same title as Moses. Sura 19:53 "And we gave him out of our mercy his brother Aaron a prophet." Just as the witness here is referred to as a messenger, taken on the title of the one whom he was sent to help. But this witness has a much greater role than Aaron. Through the messenger, The Honorable Elijah Muhammad, he was given the secrets of Allah and it is this one who is spoken of in Sura 11:1, which is none other than Farrakhan Muhammad, the same one who is sent from the original power source to bring us back into the knowledge of self so we can all live forever in the state of peace.

Sura 25:1 "Blessed is he (Allah) who sent down the Discrimination (Farrakhan) upon His servant (H.E.M) that he might be a warner to the nations."

Salâm

WHO IS YOUR MESSENGER?

The Holy Qur'an teaches that Muhammad of fourteen hundred years ago was the last prophet. Sura 33:40, says: "Muhammad is not the father of any of you men, but he is the messenger of Allah and the seal of the prophets". The word "seal" comes from the Arabic word "<u>Khā</u>tam", which means the last part or portion of a thing that is the best, this indicates finality combined with perfection and continuation of its (Qur'an) blessings.

The word "Nabiyy" is what we need to focus on here. This word is translated in English as Prophet, but the English word Prophet holds many meanings: Prophet: [Gr. Prophētēs; pro, before, and phanai, to speak] a religious teacher or leader under divine guidance; a spokesman for some cause, group, movement, etc.; a person who predicts future events in any way. So by definition we can see how many people in society today can be prophets. We have religious teachers who is inspired by God today, and people who are spokesman for certain causes, groups, movements etc.

So what exactly is the Qur'an telling us Muhammad is the seal of? In Arabic the word "Nabiyy" comes in two forms having a slight difference in meaning. "Nabiyy" without "Hamzah" and "Nabi" with "Hamzah". The difference is Nabi' with Hamzah is one who acquaints or informs others, who prophesies and is informed from God; a person who foretells, which can be one who is living right now today. Muhammad knew the different meanings of these two words.

History has it; a person came to the Holy Prophet addressing him, "Yâ Nabi' Allah", The Holy Prophet told him to say "Yâ Nabîyy Allah" (without Hamzah). Because the word "Nabîyy without Hamzah, which is the actual word used in Sura 33:40, signifies elevation and evidence of giving very big news and bringing Sharîat (Law), both words are translated in English as Prophet. But what the Qur'an is telling us here is that Muhammad was the last one to bring law, not that he was the last one who would be under divine guidance from Allah (Nabi'). There is no new law to come. The law was made complete within the Holy Qur'an; the last revelation. Thus "<u>Kh</u>âtam-al-Nabîyyîn" means the closer of the long line of those who brought law.

So Muslims today are not looking for a new law, but what about messengers. Should we be looking for a messenger? And if so, why? Many scholars try to have us believe that Muhammad was the last messenger as well. They say that Muhammad was sent as a messenger to all men on earth and therefore no more messengers are needed, and if someone comes claiming to be a messenger of Allah is a unbeliever. One of the verses in the Qur'an they use to support their teaching is Sura 34:28 which says; "And we have not sent thee but as a bearer of good news and as a warner to all mankind, but most men know not".

In this Sura we have in Arabic the words "Illâ-<u>Kh</u>âffatal-Linnâs". The word "illâ" means; except or some. This word is used to signify the sense of exception. This exception is of two kinds. The one that is used here is the exception in which the thing excepted belongs to the same class to which the things from which an exception is sought to be made belongs. As they say "Ja'al-qaumu-illa-zaidan": all the people came except Zaid (who was one of them).

Here the person Zaid belongs to the same class of people. It is called "Istithnâ' al-muttasil". So when we read verses like Sura 7:158 which has Muhammad saying, "O mankind surely I am a messenger of Allah to you all", he is not speaking about the whole human family; he is only speaking about the surrounding people of the addressed person or community whom he was among. And don't be misled by the Quranic translations like the one in Sura 4:79, that says: "And we have sent thee (Muhammad) to mankind as a messenger and Allah is sufficient as a witness." The phrase "to mankind" reads in Arabic: "Lin Nâs". The Arabic word "Li" is a preposition denoting possession and the Arabic word "Nas" means; "A people". The correct translations would be: " And we have sent thee (Muhammad) to the people as a messenger. And Allah is sufficient as a witness." Every people is to receive their own messenger. The Qur'an tells us in Sura 10:47, "and for every nation there is a messenger" in Arabic the words are "Wa-LiKhul-Li-Ummatir-rasūl".

Word for word translation: "And to all people a messenger".

The Arabic word "ummat" means; "A community; Nation; group of living things having certain characteristics and circumstances in common". So the messenger who is sent to a particular ummat (group of people) has the same characteristics of those to whom he is sent. He understands their circumstances because he is one of them. One of the most important characteristics a messenger must have of the people to whom he is sent is "language". Language is a clear indicator to whom a messenger is sent to. That is why the Qur'an tells us in Sura 14:4, "And we sent "no" messenger but with the language of "his"people.

Now we as human beings don't all speak the same language. That's why the Qur'an tells us in Sura 30:22, that one of Allah signs is the diversity of our (the human) language.

So what language did Muhammad speak, so we can be able to identify to whom he was sent to. Muhammad was an Arab who spoke Arabic. The Arabs in the Qur'an was called illiterates. Sura 62:2 says, "He it is who raised among the illiterates a messenger from among themselves". Muhammad is referred to in the Qur'an as the Ummi (illiterate) messenger. Sura 7:157 "Those who follow the messenger-prophet, the ummi (illiterate)". Remember Abraham prayer concerning the Arabs in Sura 2:129, "our Lord, and raise up in them a messenger from among them"; Sura 3:164 says, "certainly Allah conferred a favor on the believers when he raised among them a messenger from among themselves". Showing that the Arabs received an Arab as their messenger from among themselves.

If you read Sura 26: section 5-10 you will see that every people in the Qur'an received a messenger from amongst themselves, and was ordered to obey their messenger. Muhammad was an Arab sent with the language of his people, so that he might explain to them clearly. Sura 26:195 says, "In plain Arabic language". Muhammad wasn't sent to the whole world. Muhammad was only universal in the revelation in which he brought, which was the Holy Qur'an. Sura 6:19 says: "And this Qur'an has been revealed to me that with it (Qur'an) I may warn you (Arab) and who so ever it (Qur'an) reaches".

The phrase "who so ever it reaches" has two meanings. One meaning is that the Holy Qur'an is for the whole world. Sura 38:87, "It (Qur'an) is naught but a reminder to all the worlds". The second meaning is that Muhammad was sent only to warn the mother-town (Makkah) and its surrounding cities (Metropolitan). Sura 42:7, "and thus have we revealed to thee an Arabic Qur'an that thou mayest warn the mother-town (the principle city) and those around it (the whole metropolitan)". Showing that Muhammad was only sent to teach the Arabs, but the Qur'an is for the whole world.

Muhammad was only a messenger and witness for the Arab Muslims of his day and time. Muhammad is not a witness for you and I. The Qur'an tells us in Sura 16:89, "And on the day when we raise up in every people a witness against them from among themselves and bring thee (Muhammad) as a witness against these (Arabs)". This verse shows that Muhammad can only be a witness for the Muslims that he was among during his day and times. Just like every other messenger who was only a witness for those whom they were among during their lifetime. That's why the Qur'an has Jesus as saying in Sura 5:117, "I was a witness of them so long as I was among them, but when thou didst cause me to die thou wast the watcher over them". Showing that Jesus can not be a witness for those whom he was never among, likewise with Muhammad.

History has Muhammad as saying, "My Lord I can bear witness about those among whom I am living, but what about those whom I have not seen", (Ibn Kathîr). Muhammad is not the messenger raised from among ourselves, nor is he a witness for you and I today. News flash; Muhammad is Dead! So who is your messenger today?

The Qur'an says in Sura 44:1-5, that it's the book that makes things clear and that Allah are ever warning. The phrase in Sura 44:3 "every warning" in Arabic reads "Kunna-Mundhirin". The Arabic word "Kunna" is rendered to the English word "ever". The word "ever" means; always, something that is constantly or frequently recurring. And the Arabic word "Mundhir" means; "one who informs and adverse a calamity; one who cautions and put one on guard" and by attaching the letters "Ya" and "Na" shows the word in its masculine plural form. Allah is ever warning means that messengers are constantly recurring amongst the people. That's why the Qur'an says in Sura 44:5, "A command from us - truly we are every sending messengers".

So if the Qur'an is the last revelation (Law), and it is, then why send more messengers? It is because the messengers are sent to speak the language of the people in order to make plain to them the message, so you won't have an excuse to say you didn't' understand. Allah knew that if he didn't send us a messenger our excuse would be; "our Lord, why didst thou not send to us a messenger so that we might have followed thy messenger and been of the believers? (Sura 28:47). Every nation has a time when they will be destroyed for the evils in which they have done. Sura 7:34, "And every nation has a term; so when its term comes, they cannot remain behind the least while, nor can they precede it". But before Allah destroy a people he sends them a messenger to explain to them the message and warn them of the calamities that is to come. To inform the people of the march of the enemy and put them on their guard and caution them. That is why Muhammed was sent to the Arabs, he was sent to warn his people: "And we destroyed no town but it had warners to remind, and we are never unjustly" (Sura 26:28-29). Muhammad himself knew that he wasn't the last messenger. He knew that messengers would come after him to teach their people. Because he knew that evil sister nations would raise up and Allah would not destroy them without sending messengers.

Sura 28:59 says, "And the Lord never destroyed the towns until he had raised in their metropolis a messenger, reciting to them our message". Muhammad knew that Allah would do the same thing for the future generations as he did for Noah. Sura 23:31-32, "Then we raised after them another generation. So we sent among them a messenger from among them, saying serve Allah". The Qur'an also has Muhammad speaking concerning the future generations and their messengers. Sura 10:47-49 says, "And for every nation there is a messenger. So when their messenger comes, the matter is decided between them with justice , and they are not wronged".

The words "when comes" makes it very clear that this verse is referring to a future event. The English word "when" comes from the Arabic word "Idhâ" denoting future time and implying a condition. And the English word "comes" is taken from the Arabic word "Jâ'a" meaning "to come". Abdullah Yusuf Ali and others knew this verse was referring to the future, but in his translation of the Holy Qur'an he put in brackets, (was sent or came), to confuse the reader in making them think the verse is written in past tense. He is guilty of doing what the Qur'an tells us not to do; Sura 2:42, "and mix not up truth with false hood, nor hide the truth while you know". Verse 48 bear's witness that this verse is referring to the future by the question that follows; "and they say: when will this promise be fulfilled if you are truthful?"

Muhammad didn't know when this future event would take place, but he knew that every evil nation has a sister; Sura 7:38, "Every time a nation enters, it curses its sister". He knew that judgment would be taking place and therefore a messenger would be sent. Sura 17:15, "Nor do we chastise until we raise a messenger". But Muhammad didn't know exactly when this event would take place, so Sura 10:49 has Muhammad as saying: "Say: I control not for myself any harm, or any benefit except what Allah pleases. Every nation has a term". If every nation has a term that would mean every nation has a messenger. So who is your messenger? And don't say you don't have one, because the Qur'an tells us that on the day of judgment Allah will ask; "Did not there come to you messengers from among you reciting to you the message of your Lord and warning you of the meeting of this day of yours?" Then the verse goes on to show that your answer on that day will be "Yea", (Sura 39:71).

Now how will you be able to say yea if you never received a messenger from among yourselves; or did you not recognize your messengers that you deny them? (Sura 23:68). A lot of you don't know who your messengers are, that's why when the Qur'an says obey Allah and his messenger you don't know who to obey, because you don't know who your messengers are, because you're not with time. You think every time the Qur'an say obey his messenger its talking about Muhammad. Sura 4:59 says, "O you who believe obey Allah and obey the messenger and those in authority from among you". Scholars like us to believe that this is referring to Muhammad of fourteen hundred years ago.

Now if you are reading this verse relating it to the past then your correct, because the verse was revealed to the Arabs telling them (Arabs) to obey Allah and the messenger who was from among them, and Muhammad was that messenger. We must always read within time; Sura 103:1-2 says, "By the time - surely man is in loss". Everything in the Qur'an is written within time; past, present and future; and must be understood as such. If we read this same verse within time (the present) we'll be able to see the lesson it is teaching us, which is to obey Allah and the messenger and those in authority that is from among ourselves. Do you think when the Arabs of fourteen hundred years ago read Sura 26:125-126, (given the history of Hūd speaking to his people telling them) "Surely I am a faithful messenger to you: so keep your duty to Allah and obey me", that it meant they were to obey Hūd? No! The Arabs read that verse within the times understanding the history that was given about Hūd was teaching them a lesson about their messenger in relation to themselves. They knew that if they obeyed the messenger Muhammad, who was sent among themselves, they would be among those whom Allah guided, but if not they would be destroyed.

Sura 16:36 says, "And certainly we raised in every nation a messenger, saying: serve Allah and shun the devil. Then of them was he whom Allah guided, and of them was he whom remaining in error was justly due. So travel in the land, then see what was the end of the rejectors". Travel in the land means to study history. The Qur'an tells us concerning messengers of old that in their histories there is certainly a lesson for men of understanding (Sura 12:111). Every nation has its own messenger and all messengers must be obeyed. Sura 4:64, "And we sent no messenger, but that he should be obeyed by Allah's command". We must obey the messenger that is raised from among ourselves.

When we read the history of Muhammad we are not reading his history to mimic his life, in his life's history is a lesson for us to learn from. Its no different from reading the history of Lot. When we read Lot's history we don't try to mimic his life, we obtain the moral principles in which we learn from his life. To mimic Muhammad or any other messenger's life from the past would keep us out of time and not allow us room for growth and development.

Almighty God Allah, out of his mercy, raised messengers from amongst us in the day and times in which we live. Muhammad of fourteen hundred years ago is not your messenger. The word "is" is one of the six forms of "be", showing the present tense. Muhammad, Jesus, Moses, etc.; are all dead. To say that they are messengers of Allah in today's times would be incorrect. Muhammad "was" the messenger fourteen hundred years ago; "was" the past indicative of be, our language must be right and exact at all times.

I pray, that Allah help guide you to understand, and appreciate the messengers that Allah has raised from amongst ourselves right here in the wilderness of North America, The Honorable Elijah Muhammad, and his helper, Minister Farrakhan Muhammad, from the present of Allah himself to whom all praise is due forever.

Who is your messenger?

Salâm

SUNNAH

How many Muslims that are followers of the Messenger Elijah Muhammad have been told they are not true Muslims because they don't adhere to the "Sunnah of Muhammad" of fourteen hundred years ago? I don't know about you, but I have been told this several times. But I would like to say this; those who follow the Messenger Elijah Muhammad are in fact followers of the Sunnah. The difference between us and other Muslims is that we adhere to the "Sunnah" that the Holy Prophet brought, which is the "Sunnah of Allah", not Muhammad's.

Sura 33:38 of the Holy Qur'an says, "There is no harm for the Prophet in that which Allah has ordained for him. Such has been the "Way of Allah" with those who have gone before. And the command of Allah is a decree that is made absolute." The word "ordained" comes from the Arabic word "Fara_dz_" meaning; to command an observation to. The phrase "way of Allah" reads in Arabic - Sunnati-l-lâhi, Sunnah of Allah.

Sura 17:77 says, "(This is our) way with our messengers whom we sent before thee, and thou wilt not find a change in our course." According to these verses of the Qur'an we clearly see that the Sunnah is ascribed to Allah and not Muhammad.

Sura 17:77 says, "Way with our messengers whom we sent before thee." In Arabic it reads - Sunnah-man-Qad-Arsal-nā-Qab-laka-min-rusuli-nā, showing that the Sunnah Muhammad received was the same Sunnah Prophets received before him. That's why Sura 26:196 says, "And surely the same is in the scriptures of the ancients." and verse 17:77, goes on to read in Arabic, "Wa-lā-Tajid-Li-Sunnati-nā-Tahwila" - and thou will find no change in our (Allah's) Sunnah.

Sura 33:38 makes it clear that what Allah ordained for Muhammad was the "Sunnah of Allah", that which was given to all the Prophets, which shows that the Sunnah has nothing to do with the individual Prophets; but is actually the principles of Islam itself, that in which all Prophets and messengers brought that change not. Individual practice and acts of devotion among prophets and their communities change constantly.

Sura 3:50 has Jusus as saying, "And (I am) a verifier of that which is before me of the Torah, <u>and I allow you part of that which was forbidden to you</u>; and I come to you with a sign from your Lord, so keep your duty to Allah and obey me."

The Muslims of that time were followers of the practice and act of devotion of Moses, but Jesus introduced change to make it suit the needs of new times. Even though Jesus changed the practice to suit his time, the Muslims were still ordered by the Prophet Jesus to keep their duty to Allah. Because the duty of all Muslims, no matter the era, is to adhere to that which change not, the Sunnah of Allah; the Universal Principles of Islam. In Sura 16:123 Muhammad was told to follow the faith of Abraham, and followed Abraham he did, but his practice and acts of devotion wasn't that of Abraham's. For example; Muhammad established yaum al-jumu'ah the day of congregation. The time of Jumu'ah is just after noon and the service which consists only of two rak'ahs instead of four rak'ahs of the early afternoon prayer, is preceded by a sermon.

This was absolutely not the practice of Abraham. Abraham did not observe a particular day of worship. Nor did Abraham practice the numbering of rak'ahs doing prayer, such as, two rak'ahs in morning prayer or the four rak'ahs in the early afternoon prayer, ect. These practices were introduced by the Holy Prophet Muhammad. Other changes was made as well, such as the Ka'bah becoming the spiritual center for Muslims.

Sura 2:142 says in part, "The fools among the people will say: What has turned them from their qiblah which they had?" Qiblah means the direction or point towards which one turns his face (LL). In its religious usage it means the direction towards which one turns his face when saying his prayers. The change referred to here is the change which took place at Madinah about sixteen months after the prophet's flight to that city (B. 2:29). It should be noted that while the Holy Prophet was at Makkah among the idolaters of Arabia, he used to pray with his face to the Holy Temple at Jerusalem, but when he came to Madinah, where the Jewish element was strong and powerful, he was directed by Allah to turn his fact to the Ka'bah as his qiblah. But why the change?

Sura 2:143 says in part, "And we did not make that which thou wouldet have to be the qiblah but that we might distinguish him who follows the messenger from him who turns back upon his heels."

Allah implicated the change to be able to distinguish the true followers of the messenger and to know how they might act when confronted with the test of change. Sura 2:143 goes on to read, "And it was indeed a hard test except for those whom Allah has guided." It was a hard test only for those who associated the outward ceremonial practice as the true spirit of Islam. But those whom Allah guided knew that its not the outward practice that places you among the righteous. Sura 2:177 says in part, "It is not righteous that you turn your faces towards the east or the west....."

The righteous are those who follow the Sunnah of Allah, that which changes not, that in which all the Prophets and messengers of Allah taught. The belief in Allah, the last day, Angels, books of Allah, his prophets, prayer, paying the poorrate, keepers of promises, patience, feeding the needy and taking care of the orphan, and all acts of kindness, etc. All of these principles are being taught by Farrakhan Muhammad right now today. So how dare one say we, Muslims who are followers of the messenger Elijah Muhammad aren't Muslim, because we don't follow the Arab's customs and traditions of fourteen hundred years ago. I even hear Muslims who refer to their prayers as the "Sunnah Prayers", meaning they approach their prayers in the same manner as the Holy Prophet approached his prayers. But what they fail to realize is that Muhammad never referred to his outward ceremonial practice of prayer as his Sunnah.

The most authenticated Hadith of all is the Holy Qur'an itself. Sura 12:108 has Muhammad as saying, "Say: This is my way: I call to Allah, with certain knowledge - I and those who follow me." The words "This is my way" reads in Arabic, "Hâdhi-hi-sabīl", Muhammad didn't say "this is my Sunnah", he said this is my "Sabīl" meaning; his way; method; way of doing something. The words "I call to Allah" reads "Ad'û-ila-l-lâhi" meaning, "I pray to Allah" and "Alâ-Basîrtin" means; with certain knowledge. Showing that the way Muhammad prayed had a science to it. The verse goes on to say, "I and those who follow me" that's why Sura 26:217-219 says: "And rely on the Mighty, the Merciful, who sees thee (Muhammad) when thou standest up, and thy (Muhammad) movements among those who prostrate themselves." So we as Muslims who pray in the same manner as the Holy Prophet needs to understand that we are not following his Sunnah, but the Sabīl of Muhammad.

According to the Holy Qur'an, Muhammad never used such terminology (Sunnah) to describe his way of doing his prayers. Muhammad used the Arabic word "Sabīl" meaning; method or way of doing something (12:108). The "Sunnah" that Muhammad brought and gave to the Muslims of his time wasn't the "Sunnah of Muhammad", as the Qur'an teaches it was the "Sunnah of Allah" (Sura 33:38). We have to be very careful not to associate with others that which is ascribe to Allah. Sura 17:77 tells us that there will be no change in the Sunnah of Allah, so we can clearly see that the outward ceremonial practice and the Sunnah are totally two different things as taught by the Holy Qur'an. Because the "Sunnah of Allah" change not, but the acts of worship change with every nation. Sura 22:67-69 says, "To every nation we appointed acts of devotion, which they observe, so let them not dispute with thee in the matter and call to thy Lord. Surely thou art on a right guidance. And if they contend with thee say: Allah best knows what you do. Allah will Judge between you on the day of resurrection respecting that in which you differ." The words in verse 67, "To every nation we appointed acts of devotion" read in Arabic "Li-Kulli-umman-Ja'al-nā-mansakâ" the Arabic word "Ja'al means to constitute; establish. This verse clearly show how Allah allowed for every nation to set in a secure position their own acts of worship, meaning their own way of religious forms by which their reverence is expressed.

Sura 5:48 says in part, "For everyone of you we appointed a law and a way" the word "law" is taken from the Arabic word "Shir'atun" meaning the right way or mode of action; practice. The appointment of a law and a way for everyone refers to the giving of different practices to different nations in accordance with their requirements. The practice of sacrifice was shown in Moses times through the slaying of animals which is totally inappropriate in 2009. To carry out such practice today wouldn't be suitable. That is why Allah allows different nations to set up their own practices to fit the needs and times of the nation. Sura 5:101 says, "O you who believe, ask not about things which if made known to you would give you trouble; and if you ask about them when the Qur'an is being revealed, they will be made known to you. Allah pardons this; and Allah is forgiving, forbearing."

Islām discouraged rigorous practices, it also prohibited questions relating to details on many points which would require this or that practice to be made obligatory. In Islām much is left to individual will or the circumstances of the time and place. The exercise of judgment occupies a very important place in Islām, and this gives ample scope to different nations and communities to frame laws for themselves to meet new and changed situations. Just as it has been said that every generation rewrite and reinterpret it's own history, in the light of it's own experience and knowledge, so also each generation must translate and reinterpret Qur'an Majid in light of it's own experience and knowledge, where it fits and meets the requirements of the time. That's why we as Muslims should never dispute over differences in our external acts of worship.

Allah used the Jews and Christians as examples warning us Muslims of the danger of being strict in external acts while neglecting the internal purity (principle). Our external acts of worship doesn't bring us salvation, if that was the case the eastern world of Islām would be in heaven right now. Salvation comes only through true Islām (peace). And what supports Islām is its principles. If the principle of peace isn't carried out in everyday life then Islām (peace) doesn't exist.

If we say we truly believe in Allah, prayer, Zakât and fasting, etc. Then we should carry out the principles in which they represent. To go through the external forms of prayer five times a day, but not take care of the poor and the needy, isn't carrying out the principles of prayer, or giving money or food to the unfortunate, or paying the so called, Islāmic tax, but there is no purification of self, isn't carrying out the principle Zakât. To go without food from sun up to sun down, but there is no building of true discipline within self to stay away from that which is evil, isn't carrying out the principle of fasting. All of those acts are a waste if not supported by the principle, the Sunnah of Allah. So let us be true followers of the "real Sunnah" that Muhammad brought, and not get caught up in customs and traditions arguing about whose a true Muslim or not based on external practices, but let us learn to judge by the principle of Allah.

Farrakhan Muhammad said, "If one says I'm a Muslim, stop and watch how they live and that will tell you who they really are." Farrakhan is asking us to judge as Allah judges. Allah judge based on principle, not external practice.

Sura 11:117 says, "And thy Lord would not destroy the towns unjustly, while their people acted well." What we learn from this is that Allah does not destroy people unjustly; he destroys them only when they act contrary to the principle of righteousness, acting corruptly and making mischief in the land. He will not destroy them if they are "Muslihūna", right doers - whatever their beliefs or religious practice.

The Jews, Sabians and the Christians all had different practices and beliefs, but Sura 5:69 says, "Surely those who believe and those who are Jews and the Sabians and the Christians - whoever believes in Allah and the last day and does good - they shall have no fear nor shall they grieve." So let us stick to what Allah and his Holy Prophet has brought, "The Sunnah of Allah". And next time someone tells you, Muslims who are followers of the messenger Elijah Muhammad, and Farrakhan Muhammad, that you are not a true Muslim, based on the narrow-minded Mullās who on one pretext or another, issues fatwās of Kufr against this or that party of Muslims.

Just remember Sura 49:17, "They presume to lay thee under and obligation by becoming Muslims. Say: Lay me not under an obligation by your Islām; rather Allah lays you under an obligation by guiding you to the faith, if you are truthful."

Salām

HADITH

In today's times Islāmic literature is often accepted as Qur'an and Hadith. The Arabic word Hadith means; event; history and saying, the word is often times limited to the sayings, history and events of Prophet Muhammad. Due to scholar's obsession their ideas and emotions has caused compulsive preoccupation with the life of Muhammad to the point that whenever you hear terminologies such as Sunnah and Hadith you automatically associate them with the life and practice of Muhammad. When in fact the Holy Qur'an never even uses these terms in relations with Muhammad. However, when reading Hadith of any particular messenger, such as Jesus, Moses, Muhammad, ect. You are only reading their history in order to learn lessons taught through their life experience by seeing how they dealt with certain events and circumstances in their life and times. That's why Sura 12:111 says, "In their histories there is certainly a lesson for men of understanding." It didn't say "Muhammad's" history, it said their histories; meaning all the messengers of Allah.

We Muslims believe in all the messengers and Prophets of Allah, and we make no distinction between them. (Sura 2:136). The study of Hadith of all messengers are important not just the Hadith of Muhammad. Sura 79:15 asked, "Has not there come to thee the Hadith of Moses" and in verse 26 it tells us that in the Hadith of Moses is a lesson for him who fears. So why haven't Islāmic scholars written Hadith collections on Moses?

I know a lot of you haven't read the Arabic Qur'an for yourselves, and many of you didn't even know the Qur'an spoke on Hadith, because most of you rely on scholars to teach you. In their (Scholars) translations you never see the word so you assume it's not there, and you go on without knowledge because you don't ask questions and/or do investigations for yourself. A lot of Muslims are brainwashed; their taught to say, "We hear and we obey". That's not what Allah wants of us, he doesn't want us walking around brainwashed accepting things without knowledge. Sura 17:36, "And follow not that of which thou hast no knowledge. Surely the hearing and the sight and the heart, of all of these it will be asked."

Whenever knowledge is brought to us on any degree we must be intelligent enough to ask questions and then try to get to the source of the information by doing some investigations for ourselves. One of the greatest gifts Allah created is "reason". When we say we hear and we obey, it must be within reason. Sura 24:53 says, "And they swear by Allah with their strongest oaths, that if thou command them, they would certainly go forth. Say: swear not; reasonable obedience (is desired)." I ask that you use intelligence and reason concerning Hadith, because so many Muslims have been mis-educated concerning Hadiths.

When reading Hadith collections written by scholars we must understand these are not the words of Allah, and should not be accepted as such. The words of Allah stands alone and is supreme over all. So don't allow scholars to play on your intelligence by telling you that the most authentic Hadiths are the Sihāh Sittah, the six reliable works written by scholars, and that Bukhārī, (more fully, the Jāmi' of Muhammad Ismā'il al-Bukārī) is the best, most authentic. That's not true at all. Collections written by Bukārī holds some very reliable Hadiths, probably more so than Hadiths written by other scholars; but by no means do Bukārī holds the best or most authentic. The best is the word of Allah alone.

Hadiths past on from the word of mouth of men is not more authentic or reliable than Allah's word itself. Sura 39:23 says, "Allah has revealed the best Hadith, a book consistently repeating" in Arabic it reads, "Allahu-nazzala-Ahsana-l-Hadith-Kitâban-Mutashābihan-Mathani". This verse clearly tells us that the best Hadith is the Holy Qur'an. The book that is consistent. Hadiths collections written by scholars are not consistent, they have Hadiths, which scholars say themselves, is weak and unsound. For example, "Busr ibn sa'īd related, Zaid ibn Khālid spoke to him, while with Busr ibn sa'īd was 'Ubaid Allāh, that Abū Talhah related to him that the prophet (PBUH) said, "Angels do not enter a house in which is an image." (B.59:7)

Sūrah means an image or a picture. According to another version (B.59:7), the Holy Prophet is reported to have said that "Angels do not enter a house in which is a dog or a Sūrah." But, the Holy Qur'an allows the keeping of dogs (5:4) and so does Hadith (H.28:8); and the keeping of watch dogs is also allowed. Similarly, the Holy Qur'an speaks of tamāthīl (images) being made for Solomon, and it would not be right to say that angels did not on this account come into the house of Solomon, a prophet of Allah. The Hadith, which speaks of angels not visiting a place where images (or pictures) and dogs are to be found cannot be accepted, and if so not in its literal sense.

The Holy Qur'an is all authentic and sound; it's the best. The Qur'an tells us in Sura 39:18,55 to follow the best. So if the Qur'an is the best, and it is, then what Hadith will you believe in after Allah and his signs? (Sura 45:6). Why would you continue to look for something else other than the Qur'an? Sura 29:51 says, "Is it not enough for them that we have revealed to thee the book (Qur'an) which is recited to them?" The Hadith that Allah revealed wasn't enough, so what did they do, those who rejected the Qur'an alone? They created their own Hadiths. But Allah knew this would happen, that's why Allah warned us against "Lahwa-L-Hadith". Sura 31:6 says, "And of men is he who takes instead frivolous Hadiths to lead astray from Allah's path without knowledge and to make it (Qur'an) a mockery." The word "frivolous" is taken from the Arabic word "Lahw", meaning "way causing diversion".

Hadiths written by scholars is what has the Muslim community divided today. Sura 30:32, "of those who split up their religion and become parties; every sect rejoicing in that which is with it." Shi'ites rejoicing over "Ali and their 12 Imams, as the Sunnies rejoice over the four Khalifas and their reliable scholars of their choice, Sihāh Sittah. Each community has their own Hadith collections to support whatever it is they teach. Sura 68:37-38 says, "or have you a book wherein you read that you shall surely have therein what you choose?" Allah tells us to stay away from sects, Sura 6:159 says, "As for those who split up their religion and become sects, thou hast no concern with them. Their affair is only with Allah, then he will inform them of what they did." Allah will not allow such persons to get away. Sura 68:44 says, "So leave me alone with him who rejects this (Qur'an) Hadith. We shall overtake them by degrees from whence they know not." The unbelievers never accepted the Qur'an alone they always wanted something else alone with it they even tried to get Muhammad to change it or to make-up something else to go alone with it, but Muhammad never gave in.

Sura 17:73-74 says, "And surely they had purposed to turn thee (Muhammad) away from that which we have revealed to thee, that thou shouldst forge against us other than that (Qur'an) and then they would have taken thee for a friend. And if we had not made thee firm, thou mightiest have indeed inclined to them a little." But Muhammad stayed firm, Sura 10:15 says, "And when our clear messages are recited to them, those who have no hope of meeting with us say: Bring a Qur'an other than this or change it. Say: It is not for me to change it on my own accord. I (Muhammad) follow naught but what is revealed to me."

The Holy Prophet warned them by the teaching of Qur'an alone, that's why Sura 21:45 says, "Say: I warn you only by revelation." That's why we as Muslims should never accept Hadiths outside of the Holy Qur'an, unless they are confirmed by the Qur'an itself. Sura 42:24 says, "Allah blots out the falsehood and confirms the truth with his words." If a Hadith, written by scholars are in fact true, then the Qur'an will confirm its truths. However, we as Muslims should always make our final decision based on the word of Allah. Sura 6:149 says, "Say: Then Allāh's is the conclusive argument:"

Sura 6:155, "And this is a book we have revealed, full of blessings; so follow it (Qur'an) and keep your duty that mercy may be shown to you."

Sura 15:9, "Surely we have revealed the reminder, and surely we are its guardian."

The Qur'an is frequently called Dhikr, and "Ahl al-Dhikr" are Muslims who are followers of the Qur'an and keepers of the Oracles of Allah. The messenger Elijah Muhammad said, the Holy Qur'an Sharrieff is the book that make things clear, and it also gives to us the perfect rule and guidance. As long as we adhere to the Holy Qur'an we can never go wrong. So let us do as Allah commands, "remind by means of the Qur'an him who fears my threat." (Sura 50:45)

Salām

HADITH EXAMPLES

In the previous chapter I eradicated the idea of accepting Hadi<u>th</u>s written by scholars of Islam, even though they provide a very wide and comprehensive collection of information on the history of the Holy Prophet Muhammad, and some of these Hadi<u>th</u>s are very helpful. But Hadi<u>th</u>s should only be accepted when supported by the Holy Qur'an itself. So here I offer a few Hadi<u>th</u>s that corroborates with the Qur'an, so you the reader, can learn how to reference the principles of Hadi<u>th</u>s back to the Qur'an in order to substantiate its validations of assertions. May Allah bless you with understanding as you continue to read.

Abū Hurairah reported that The Prophet, (PBUH), said: "Religion is easy, and no one exerts himself too much in religion but it overpowers him; so act aright and keep to the mean, and be of good cheer and ask for (Divine) help at morning and at evening and during a part of the night." (B.2:29).

This Hadi<u>th</u> shows what the Islamic conception of religion is. Religion does not consist in performing to many devotional exercises; these are in fact discouraged as they ultimately overpower the man who indulges in them. Religion is the name of acting aright and keeping to the mean course; this would keep a man in good heart (mind), (MMA). "And strive hard for Allah with due striving. He has chosen you and has not laid upon you any hardship in religion." (Holy Qur'an 22:78)

'A'i<u>sh</u>ah reported that the Prophet, (PBUH), entered upon her and with her was a woman. He asked, "Who is this?" (A'i<u>sh</u>ah) said, she is such and such a one; and began to speak (highly) of her prayers. He said: "Enough; only that is binding on you which you are able to do; by Allah, Allah does not get tired but you get tired, and the devotions dearest to him are those in which the devotee preservers. (B.2:31) Only that is binding on you which you are able to do is supported by Sura 6:152, which says: "We impose not on any soul a duty except to the extent of its ability." The chief aim of religion is, as made clear in the concluding words of this Hadith, to bring about perseverance in the character of a man. He is, therefore, told to adopt that course in religious devotion in which he can keep constant. "Peace be to you, because you were constant." (Holy Qur'an 13:24)

'Abd Allah ibn 'Amr reported, the Messenger of Allah, (PBUH), said to me, "O 'Abd Allah! Am I not told that thou fastest in the day time and standest up in devotion during the night?" I said, yes, O Messenger of Allah. He said: "Do not do so; keep fast and break it and stand up in devotion and have sleep, for thy body has right over thee, and thine eye has aright over thee, and thy wife has right over thee, and the person who pays thee a visit has right over thee." (B.30:55).

There are many versions of this Hadith and in all of them it is made clear by the Holy Prophet that a man has several duties to perform and he must keep all of them in mind in devoting himself to religious exercise. No religious exercise, whether it is keeping the fast or standing up in prayer, will do him good if he neglects his worldly duties. In fact, religious devotion is meant to make a man fitter for the performance of his duties, which he own to others.

In the development of his spiritual, the physical side and worldly duties are not to be neglected. (MMA). "And seek the abode of the hereafter by means of what Allah has given thee, and neglect not thy portion of the world." (Holy Qu'ran 28:77). One who truly remembers Allah much, is one who is kind to humanity. Sura 107 says; "Hast thou seen him who belies religion? That is the one who is rough to orphan, and urges not the feeding of the needy. So woe to the praying ones, who are unmindful of their prayer! Who do (them) to be seen, and refrain from acts of kindness! "Being unmindful of prayer mean not paying heed to the spirit of prayer, which is described in the two previous verses as being the help of the orphan and the needy.

Prayer to Allah and help of the poor are repeatedly spoken of in the Holy Qur'an as the two foundations of Islam, but here we are told that even prayer is a mere show, if it does not generate feelings (acts) of love and sympathy for humanity. That's why the Holy Qur'an says in Sura 4:142, "And when they stand up for prayer, they stand up sluggishly - they do it only to be seen of men and remember Allah but little."

'Abd Allah ibn 'Amr reported, a Messenger of Allah, (PBUH), what Islam is the best? He said: "That thou feed (the poor) and offer salvation to whom thou knowest and whom thou dost not know." (B.2:5)

Nu'mān ibn Bashir said, I heard the messenger of Allah, (PBUH), say; "What is lawful is manifest and what is unlawful is manifest and between these two are doubtful things which many people do not know.

So whoever guards himself against the doubtful things, he keeps his religion and his honor unsullied, and whoever falls into doubtful things is like the herdsman who grazes his cattle on the borders of a reserve - he is likely to enter it. Know that every king has a reserve (and) know that the reserve of Allah in his land is what he has forbidden. Know that in the body there is a bit of flesh; when it is sound the whole body is sound, and when it is corrupt the whole body is corrupt. Know it is the heart." (B.2:38).

The first part of this Hadith is support by Sura 2:256, which says: "The right way is indeed clearly distinct from error." The man who is imbued with a truly religious spirit avoids not only what is manifestly unlawful, but even the doubtful things which might lead him into the unlawful.

The concluding portion the Hadith shows that religion does not consist in the devotional exercises which a man may perform, but in the presence in him of aright mentality - the mentality to act aright and avoid the wrong. (MMA). A sound mind is of the essence of religion, as the Holy Qur'an says: "Except him who comes to Allah with a sound heart (mind)."

As you can see, these Hadiths mentioned above are all supported by the Holy Qur'an. These are the kinds of Hadiths written by scholars that you should accept, because the truth of them is confirmed by the Holy Qur'an. Now I would like to list a few Hadiths that are not supported by the Holy Qur'an and show why they should not be accepted. As well as those that the Qur'an refers to as, "Lahwa-L-Hadith ", frivolous Hadith .

'Ā' ishah said, I used to comb the hair of the mesenger of Allah, (PBUH). (B.6:2). 'Ā' ishah said, I used to perfume the Prophet, (PBUH), with the best fragrant substance which he could find. So much so that I could discern the brightness of the fragrance in his head and in his beard. (B.77:74).

These Hadiths that was just recited are totally frivolous (Lahw), trivial, insignificant; no subsistence what so ever. Knowing about the perfume of Muhammad and how 'Ā' ishah combed his hair is not conducive or beneficial at all. To preoccupy ones self with such Hadiths leads into obsession, and obsession leads to the worship of Muhammad, which is shirk, which many Muslims are already guilty of today. "And of men is he who takes instead frivolous Hadith to lead astray from Allah's path without knowledge (Holy Qur'an 31:6).

Abū Hurairah reported on the authority of the Prophet, (PBUH), that he forbade the wearing of a gold ring. (B.77:45), Hudhaifah said, I heard the Prohet, (PBUH), say: "Do not wear silk or silk brocade, and do not drink in vessels of gold and silver and do not eat in bowls made of them; for they are for them in this life and for us in the next." (B.70:29). In the Hadiths just mentioned above Muhammad was reported to have said that the wearing of gold and silk is foreboded because these things are for the believers in the next meaning, the garden; paradise. Some scholars accept this Hadith as sound base on Sura 22:23 which says; "Surely Allah will make those who believe and do good deeds enter gardens wherein flow rivers - they are adorned therein with bracelets of gold and (with) pearls. And their garments therein are of silk." If we accept this Qur'anic verse in its literal sense and these Hadiths as truth, as some scholars do, it means that we have to start teaching that its foreboding to wear silver, pearls, to possess drinking - cups, and to even have carpet and couches in our homes.

Sura 76:12-22, mentioned all thee above as being given to the believers in the gardens. Such teaching would be absurd! The Holy Qur'an clearly tells us that the description of the garden and all that it contains is no more than a parable. Sura 47:15 says: "A parable of the garden which the dutiful are promised: therein are rivers of water." And this same verse also mentions milk and honey, and we know milk and honey isn't forbading. The fact of the matter is that the blessings of paradise cannot be conceived in this present life, and are not therefore things of this present world.

An explanation of these words by the Holy Prophet is given in Bukhāri as follows: "Allah says, I have prepared for my righteous servants what no eye has seen and no ear has heard, and what the mind of man has not conceived." (B.59:8), This Hadith is supported by the Holy Qur'an 32:17 which says: "No soul knows what refreshment of the eyes is hidden for them: a reward for what they did."

The gifts of the Garden is given to the righteous in the hereafter, here on earth after the wicked rule of Satan. When the righteous activities and conditions is in total compliance to the will of Allah. Only then will you be able to experience the mercy of Allah on its highest level. In this present state of condition ones mind can't even fathom the gifts of the blessing of paradise. That's why Ibn 'Abbas is reported to have said that "nothing that is in paradise resembles anything that is in this (present) world except in name." (RM, Vol. 1, p.172).

For instance, the word zill (lit., shade) occurs very often in the Holy Qur'an in connection with the blessings of paradise, but a shade is not what is really meant: for there is no sun: "they will see therein neither sun nor intense cold." (Qur'an 76:13). The word is there but the significance underlying it is different. And this goes for, the milk, the honey, the cushions, the thrones, the clothes and the adornments of the gardens: these descriptions are of the nature of similes as the Qur'an expressly calls them a mathal - simile or parable. The Holy Qur'an does not forbade the wearing of gold or any other item mention above, such Hadiths is to be rejected.

I pray that Allah bless you with understanding.

Salām

THE DEVIL/JINN

The Messenger Elijah Muhammad taught us that the black man is the original man, and that the black man is righteous by nature. Why did Elijah Muhammad make color a subject of interest? What does the color of man has to do with his spiritual advancement? Did Allah actually reveal such teachings to Elijah Muhammad? In the "Message to the Blackman", page 320, on whites as "Devils" Elijah Muhammad said: "it's what he revealed, and what he revealed is what I am teaching and believe in and this term "Devil" or name "Devil" is applied to wicked people (people who are wicked by nature). They were made white or a different color because they had been grafted out of the darker people, and therefore they have that color.

Does the Qur'an bear witness to such teachings? Does the Qur'an teach that the black man is the original man; or that a people was really created out of another race of people, and that a people was really created evil by nature? Let's go to the Qur'an and see what it has to say concerning these teachings.

Sura 45:4, tells us there are signs in our creation and the signs are for a people who are sure. Sura 30:22, tells us that there are even signs in our colors, which shows that we are to gain a certain knowledge by studying the diversity of mankind, but only those who will understand the lessons are those who are learn.

The word "learn" is taken from the Arabic word "Alimî" (plu) meaning: those having knowledge to distinguish. This shows that only those who are wise enough to distinguish between the colors of the races of man will understand the lesson. The word lesson is taken from the Arabic word "Mutawassimîn" which means; those who can interpret and read the sign; the intelligent ones (15:75). So why does the society we live in tells us that color doesn't mean anything, and that we should be color blind, and when anyone teach on the difference of the colors of mankind they are hated. Why?

The Qur'an says that in our color are signs. The word "sign" comes from the Arabic word "Ayat". A sign is a general term for anything that gives evidence of an event, a mood, a quality of character, a mental or physical state, or a trace of something. Let's go to the Qur'an and see what it has to say concerning the Black man. In the Qur'an, Sura 32:7, it says, "He who made beautiful everything that he created, and he began the creation of man from dust." Now what are the signs here? The word "beautiful" is taken from the Arabic word "Ahsana", which means; good; excellent. The word "began" is taken from the Arabic word "Bada'a", which means; originated, and the word "dust" is from the Arabic word "Tîn" meaning "mud" which is a wet soft earthy matter. So what the Qur'an is telling us here in 32:7, is that everything Allah originated was good by nature which is the innate or essential qualities or character that it was given from it's creation.

The original man here, is said to have originated from mud which is earthy matter mixed with water; water is the source and cause of all life. Sura 21:30, in part says, " we made from water everything living" and the texture of mud is soft. The word "soft" means; easily impressible; the contrary of hard; not rought, rude or violent. So the sign in the softness of the mud is showing the mood state of mind, inclination and disposition of the original man who is being created.

Sura 15:26 says, "And surely we created man of sounding clay, of black mud fashioned into shape".

Arabic Translation: "S̲als̲âlim-min-hama-im-masnûn".

Verse 28 of the same Sura gives even more information concerning the original man here by using the word "Bashar". The Arabic word "Bashara" means, "skin; the outer and visible part of the skin; human body, person". "S̲als̲âl" means, "Dry ringing clay; clay that emits a sound, and "hama" means; black mud. Lastly, "masnûn" means; formed, made into shape.

So what is actually being created here is the original human body (Bashar), that emits sound (S̲als̲âl), which shows that the original material of the human body is from the earth. It's a sonorous body having the sensation of sound, and the dryness is showing that it (the body) is without water, which symbolize life. It's only when water is mixed with the clay of the earth that it becomes mud; only when water is present could life be produced. "We made from water everything living". Hama' shows the color of the body that is being created here is black. So we can clearly see from these verses of the Qur'an that the original man that was created here was the black man.

So if the original man was black, where and how did the other colors of man come about? Sura 35:27 says, "Seest thou not that Allah sends down water from the clouds, then we bring forth therewith fruits of various hues? And in the mountains are streaks, white and red, of various hues and (others) intensely black".

Now this is the translation by Maulana Muhammad Ali, and you will find similar translations in most Qur'ans'. This translation is in fact true, but only on the surface. You have to read this verse in Arabic to understand its deeper significance.

In Arabic it reads, "A'Lam tara-anna-Allah-Anzala-min-Samâ'i-mâ'an-fa-A<u>kh</u>raina-Be-hi-<u>Th</u>amara-Mu<u>kh</u>talifan-Alwân-hâ-wa-min-Al Jibâl-Judad-Bîdza-<u>h</u>umr-Mu<u>kh</u>talifun-Alwân-hâ-wa-<u>Gh</u>arâbîb-Sûdun".

Word for word translation: "Behold indeed Allah sent down from heaven water and brought from it a fruit one of various colors, also in the mighty people are tracks, white and red, one of various colors but jet black are the great people".

This verse tells us that out of mâ'an (water) Allah A<u>kh</u>raj (brought forth) <u>Th</u>amara (singular)(a fruit) and that this one fruit contained within itself many colors (Alwân). Now the Arabic word "Alwân" that is translated to color, also means "external form; species, kind, race", which is the meaning when associated with the Arabic word "Al-Jibâl". The word "Al-Jibâl" is where the word "mountains" is taken from, but the word "Jibâl" actually means; Chiefs; Lords; mighty persons. Another one of it's forms is "Jibillan", which means; generations. So we can clearly see that this word is referring to people. When translated as mountain, it is used as a metaphor.

When the Qur'an speaks of mountains in its lateral sense, it always use the Arabic word "rawâsîya". The Arabic word "G̱harâbîb" means; extremely black, raven black. The word "Sûdun" is the (n. plu) of "muswaddan", which means; great people; black ones. So what the Qur'an is telling us here in Sura 35:27, is that these mighty people contained within themselves various species or kinds (races), ranging from the colors of white through red, the colors in between are yellow and brown. And this same verse tells us that the great people are the black people, showing that these might persons was nonother than the original black man who gave birth to all of the other races of the human family.

The Qur'an also bears witness that there were a people who was created out of another race of people in Sura 6:133, which reads, "And thy Lord is the self-sufficient one, the Lord of mercy. If he please, he may remove you, and make whom he please successors after you, even as he raised you up from the seed of other people". In Arabic the words "even as he raised you from the seed of other people" reads, "Kamâ-Ansha-Kum-min-D̲hurriyyat-Qaum-Ak̲harin".

The word "Kamâ" means; just as; and the word "Ansha" means; to create; produced. The word "Kum" means; you; and the word "min" is a proposition that is used for expressing a starting point; showing origin. "Dhurriyyat" means; decents; race. "Quam" means; a people; and "Akharîn" means; another. A more clearer translation would be, "Just as he created you from another race of people". Now who are these people that came from another race of people? Does the Qur'an give more information about such people? Do they have a different nature and color from the original people?

In order to understand such truth you have to first understand the Jinn. The Qur'an speaks about the Jinn throughout the Qur'an, but exactly who or what are Jinns? Some scholars say that Jinns are imaginary beings whom the infidels worshipped, evil spirits. Others say they are people of different far flung countries living detached from civilized people. People who inherited the earth in prehistoric times; subjected to no laws or rules of conduct.

Ibn Manzûr in his dictionary Lisân al-'Arab show that Jinns are people. Zuhair ibn Abî Sulmâ says Jinns are people who are peerless, having no match or equal. But what exactly does the Qur'an say about the Jinn. Let's see......

Sura 46;29 says, "and when we turned towards thee a party of the Jinn, so when they were in its presence, they said: Be silent. Then when it was finished, they turned back to their people warning (them)". The word "party" was taken from the Arabic word "Nafaran", which means; people, company not exceeding ten nor less then three, showing that it was three to ten people of the Jinns who listened to the Qur'an. After listening to the Qur'an they went back to their "Quam", which means; tribe, people. So the Qur'an clearly tells us that the Jinns are a people.

When you read the story of Solomon you will see that it was these same people whom Solomon employed to do the work of building and diving. It was these same people Solomon referred to as the devils. Sura 34:12 says in part, "And of the Jinn there were those who worked before him by the command of his Lord. And who ever turned aside from our command from among them, we made him taste of the chastisement of burning".

The Jinn were people whom Solomon subjected to his rule and forced into service by his Lords command. Notice that the Jinn of this verse is the same people Solomon called Shayātin (devils) in 38:37, "The devils, every builder and diver" and Sura 21:81 says, "And of the devils there were those who dived for him and did other work besides that: and we kept quard over them". The word "devil" comes from the Arabic word "Shayātin", its root is "Shatana" which means; to be obstinate, perverse, become remote or far from the truth and from the mercy of God. The word "Shayātin" means, a person who is not only himself far from the truth but also turns others away from it: who burns with hatred and anger and is lost. Shayātin is used in the Qur'an to refer to the leader, rebellious, noisy, evil, troublesome person. And Solomon tells us that these people wasn't just evil but that they were evil by "nature".

Sura 27:39 says in part, "one audacious among the Jinn said..." in Arabic it reads, "Qâ la 'Ifrîtun min Al-Jinn". The word "Audacious" was taken from the Arabic word "Ifrîtun", which means: daemon; one evil by nature. This meaning gives us a better understanding of Sura 15:27 which says, "And the Jinn, we created before of intensely hot fire". The word fire comes from the Arabic word "Nâra" which means; to emit fire or light; vex or provoke war.

Maulana Muhammad Ali's commentary to Sura 15:27 says in part, "In man's creation from dust there also seems to be a refrence to his low and humble origin and to his temperate nature, as opposed to another kind of creation of a fiery nature, which is called the Jinn or the devil. The two words, Jinn and Devil, are frequently applied to men of a fiery temperament or rebellious nature, men who lead others to evil". The Qur'an supports Maulana's interpretation.

Sura 2:102 says, "And they follow what the devils fabricated against the Kingdom of Soloman", devils here means human devils. Sura 72:6 says, "and person from among men used to seek refuge with persons from among the Jinn, so they increased them in evil doing". The Jinn here are nonother than the devils, the leaders of evil. The men here refer to people who are of a different race from the Jinn, but was made weaker in intellect and followed the Jinns blindly.

Sura 6:128 says in part, "O assembly of Jinn, you took away a great part of men". We see from reading this verse that it is the Jinn who lead away a great part (85%) of men to evil. The word "assembly" is taken from the Arabic word "Ma'Shara" means; race, a tenth part. This shows that this race of Jinns are the tenth part (10%er's) who leads away the majority of mankind. It's these people who are referred to as the decendants of Iblīs, the devil himself. Let's read the hisotry of Iblis as told by the Qur'an.

Sura 2:30, tells us that Allah was going to place a ruler in the earth and the angels asked why would you place in it one who would cause mischief and shed blood? But how could the angels ask such question if they had no knowledge of mischief and the shedding of blood? Verse 32, tells us that the angels had no knowledge, but what Allah has taught them. So did Allah teach them about blood shed and mischief?

The one who was placed in the earth to rule is referred to as a "Khalîfah", which means; successor; one who take the place of another. Khalîfah comes from the root word "Khalafa", which means; to be altered, corrupt, disobey, transgress. So we can see that this one who was placed in the earth to rule would transgress and disobey at some point. It was through the languish in itself that the angels knew that this one would be evil, and its this same one who disobeyed Allah in verse 34, whom Allah referred to as "Iblīs". Iblīs is the one who was placed to be ruler in Sura 2:30. Iblīs means: person of desperate character.

Masûd and Ibn'Abbas explain the word K͟halîfah as the one who judges among or rules the people of God by his command. And it's this same one who Allah called S͟haytan in verse 36, who cause man to fall from his natural state. The same verse tells us that Iblīs and his race are enemies to the original man. Iblīs felt that he was better than the black man, those who was created from black mud.

Sura 7:12 has Iblīs as saying "I am better than he, thou hast created me of fire, while him thou didst create of dust". The original man was created from dust which stands for humility and meekness, showing that the original man's nature is humble and meek. But Iblīs nature is nâra. Nâra means; to emit fire; to irritate; make war. In Arabic literature and in the Holy Qur'an "nâra" is often a symbol of war. Nâra, as you can see, also means to irritate. Irritate means; to inflame or chafe; inflame is to kindle or arouse. Kindle is to stir up , to wake up from or as if from sleep. This is exactly what Iblīs did causing the original man to fall from his original state.

Sura 7:20, tells us how the devil kindle and arouse up that which was hidden within the original man by evil suggestion causing him to fall. The devil is always seeking to destroy the original man, he knows that the original man is the people of God. He knows that the original man is greater than the universe itself.

Iblīs was placed in the earth to rule for a period of time, but yet Allah asked him to submit to Adam (the original Adam).

You think the devil liked that? No he didn't! Listen to his attitude towards the original man, so you can see just how much he hates you. Sura 17:62, has Iblīs as saying, "This is he whom thou hast honored above me! If thou respite me to the day of resurrection, I will certainly cause his progeny to perish except a few". But how will Iblīs deceive the original man? What are his methods?

Sura 17:64 says, "And incite whom thou canst of them with thy voice. And collect against them thy horse and thy foot, and share with them in wealth and children, and promise them. And the devil promises them only to deceive". So we learned here that the devil will use his voice to incite the original man. The word "incite" comes from the Arabic word "Istafziz", which means; to deceive, lead to destruction, make weak by humiliating. The Phares, "collect against them they horse and thy foot" is a metaphor signifying the use of ones power and might.

The devil used all of his power and might to humiliate the original man by the treatment in which he took the original man through; weakening his spirit, leading him to destruction by teaching him contrary of Allah. Blinding him by sharing with them in wealth and children. The original man is so blind deaf and dumb now that he measures his success and accomplishments based on the wealth and benefits that the devil allows him to obtain; allowing him the freedom to mate and associate with the devil's children without interference.

Deceiving the original man so bad that he now befriends the devil because of benefits calling him (the devil) his friend.

Sura 6:128 tells us that on the day of judgment the greater part of the original man (85%er's) will say, "Our Lord, some of us profited by others (the Jinn) and we have reached our appointed term which thou didst appoint for us". What is appointed for them was told to us in Sura 17:63, which says, "Begone! Whoever of them follows thee surely hell is your recompense a full recompense". The Qur'an clearly tells us that whoever follow Iblīs and his children will be destroyed with the devil. Sura 15:43 says, "And surely hell is the promised place for them all". Iblīs knew he would be successful in deceiving the greater part (85%) of the original man, that is why he said with such confidence, "I shall cause them all to deviate, except thy servants from among them, the purified ones". (Sura 15:39-40).

The purified ones are the 5%er's, who soars with the higher spiritual region and is not bent low upon earthly things. The few, 5%er's, knows who the true and living God Allah is and can't be deceived by the devil's voice (teachings) power, wealth and children. The poor righteous teachers adhere to the teachings of Allah himself. They do not adhere to the devil nor his children, nor do they take them for friends. Allah asked a question in Sura 18:50, "Will you then take him (Iblīs) and his offspring for friends rather than me, and they are your enemies?" These people, the Jinns, are the natural enemy to the original Adam (man); we must understand this.

Sura 36:60-62 says, "Did I not charge you, O children of Adam that you serve not the devil? Surely he is your open enemy. And that you serve me. This is the right way. And certainly he led astray numerous people from among you. Could you not then understand?" The enemy said he would deceive the original man with his voice which represent his teachings. But what teaching did the Jinn use that made him so successful in deceiving the world? The Jinn created a false relationship between himself and Allah. Sura 37:158 says, "And they assert a relationship between him (Allah) and the Jinn". The word "relationship" is taken from the Arabic word "Nasaba" which means; to show ones genealogy or linage.

The Jinn teaches that he is the <u>Son of Allah,</u> claiming a direct linage; teaching people that when they worship the son they are in fact worshipping Allah. But in actuality they are worshipping the Jinn. In order to identify the Jinn all one has to do is just look at the image of the Son of God that the world is worshipping, because that is actually the image of the Jinns themselves. Sura 34:40-41 says, "And on the day when he will gather them all together, then will he say to the angels: Did those worship you? They will say: Glory be to thee! Thou art our protecting friend, not they: nay, they worship the Jinn; most of them were believers in them". The image of the son of God that the Jinns represented to the world is the same image of the evil people that the Qur'an say would be let loose in the world to control with evil.

Sura 21:96 says, "Even when Gog and Magog are let loose and they sally forth from every elevated place". The Arabic words "Yâjûj" (Gog) and "Mâjûj" (magog) are derived from the root word "Ajja", which refers to the scythians of the fartheset east and all of the Caucasian nations inhabiting the North of Asisan and in Europe. The Sacae are the teutons an ancient caucasian people of germanic or celtic origin who lived in Jutland unitl about 100 B.C., and the Slau is a caucasion— slavic speaking people of eastern Europe. Gog and Magog are nonother than the caucasian people of Europe and North of Asia.

The caucasian history was given in Sura 18, and under different names all throughout the Holy Qur'an. Elijah Muhammad teaches us that the devils were in heaven causing trouble amongst the righteous. Elijah said, the devil(s) made trouble for six months right in heaven. The Holy Qur'an bears witness to the teachings of Elijah Muhammad when properly understood. But in order to understand this fact, one must first come to understand that heaven is not a place, but a condition.

Sura 57:21 says, "Vie one with another forgiveness from your Lord and a garden the extensiveness of which is as the extensiveness of the heaven and the earth—it is prepared for those who believe in Allah and his messengers"....The garden or the Paradise "(heaven) is here said to be as extensive as the heavens and the earth, and a similar statement occurs in Sura

3:133. These statements afford us the key to a right conception of paradise.

The following incident is related under Sura 3:133, "A messenger of Heraclius asked the Holy Prophet: If Paradise were as extensive as the heavens and the earth, where would be Hell?" the Holy Prophet replied "Glory be to Allah!" where is the night when the day comes? (RZ) it shows clearly that heaven and hell are not the names of two places, but are really two conidtions; because if paradise were the names of a particular place, hell could not exist as paradise would, according to these verses extend over the whole of space". It is this heavenly state that the original man was in before he was decived by the devil. He lived on the best part of the earth's land the Eastern part, which was referred to as the garden as well.

Sura 2:35 says, "and we said: O Adam, dwell thou and thy wife in the Garden, and eat from it a plenteous (food) wherever you wish, and approach not this tree, lest you be of the unjust." the word "Garden" comes from the Arabic word "jinnah", which means, "Paradise". It's not an imaginary place out in space somewhere, paradise is right here on earth, it's a life of comfort, ease and happiness. While in the Garden the original man was ordered to keep away from the tree, but what exactly is this tree?

In Sura 20:120, the devil said that it was "the tree of immortality", but in actuality it was just the opposite of what the devil state it to be. It was the tree of death, the spriritual death of man that comes by way of the devil's teaching (voice). The devil teaches the original man to think and act contrary to the teachings of Allah, and such way of teaching is evil. Sura 14:26, tells us that an evil word is likned to "an evil tree pulled up from the earth's surface; it has no stability". This tree represents the devil and his teachings. Sura 3:62, calls it the tree of "zaggūm".

The word zaggūm means; deadly food; food which kills, which represent the spritual food (teaching) that we eat of the devil. Sura 44:43-44 says, "Surely the tree of zaggūm is the food of the sinful". Sura 37:64-65 says, "It is a tree that grows in the bottom of hell its produce is as it were the heads of serpents (devils)". The word hell comes from the Arabic word "Ja<u>h</u>im", which means; blazing fire; intense fire. Ja<u>h</u>im comes from the root word "Ja<u>h</u>ama", which means; to light and stir up the fire, open the eyes to evil". That's exactly what the devil did when he made manifest to them of their shame (Sura 7:20). The word shame comes from the Arabic word "Sau'at" it signifies any saying or action of which or is ashamed when exposed to view, or any evil. The devil knew if he could get the original man to think evil thoughts that he (the devil) could alter the nature of the original man; placing him in hell! By turning him into that which Allah never intended him to be, a devil.

The devil said in Sura 4:119, "And certainly I will lead them astray and excite in them vain desires and bid them so that they will slit the ears of the cattle, and bid them so that they will alter Allah's creation". Farrakhan taught us how devils are made. He said it starts with a wrong though coming up in the mind. Once the devil got us to think evil the act followed. Even though the devil wasn't successful in completely changing the original man's nature, he was successful in reversing the natural roads within the original man, by suppress the good, and activating the evil that which laid dormant, turning the original man into a devil.

Sura 30:30 says, " there is no altering Allah's creation". The word "altering" is taken from the Arabic word "Tabdîlan", which means; permutation. Elijah Muhammad said, "We have become like those devils in so many ways, but we are not by nature evil or unrighteous." Farrakhan says, we are black devils today, and I agree. We are not devils by the nature in which Allah created us in, but we have become devils by our ways an actions. "This is why Allah says there are devils among men and Jinn." (Sura 6:112)

It was a time when you could identify the devil by color alone, but that is not the case today. Elijah Muhammad told us how to distinguish a devil is by carefully watching their behavior. But the original man has followed the devil so closely that studying the behavior of the two people today you can't tell the difference. The original man has taken on the characteristics of the serpent, his ways and actions is that of a grafted snake. Now we, the original people, have to get back to the nature in which Allah has created us, where the evil is suppressed and the good is dominate. The devil has caused us to depart from that sate in which we were in; we have to learn from our father's history.

Allah tells us in Sura 7:27, "O children of Adam, let not the devil seduce you, as he expelled your parents from the garden". The devil deceived our parents causing them to fall, but once they learned just who was causing trouble, they cast the trouble makers out of paradise. Sura 2:36 says, "But the devil made them slip from it, and caused them to depart from the state in which they were. And we said: Go forth, some of you are the enemies of others. And there is for you in the earth and abode and a provision for a time." The words "go forth" is taken from the Arabic word "Ibiṯû", which means; go forth from this state; go to some town; get down from this land. This shows that the devils was made to leave the best part of the earth, "Firdaus" fertile land; the best place of paradise. But where did they go?

According to the word of Allah the devils were driven from the Garden of Paradise into the hills and caves of West Asia, or as they now call it, "Europe". They were without anything to start civilization, they were punished by being deprived of divine guidance for 2000 years which brought them almost into the family of wild beasts. The Qur'an tells us in Sura 18:18, that if you would have seen them in such condition you would have been filled with awe because of them. And it is these same people that the Qur'an tells us are the enemies of the original man. That is why they were driven ouf of paradise into the hills of West Asia (Europe). Once they were there, they were roped in to keep them out of paradise from causing trouble.

The Qur'an says in Sura 18:94-97, "They said; O Dhu-l-garnain, Gog and Magog do mischief in the land. May we then pay thee tribute on condition that thou raise a barrier between us and them? He said: that werein my Lord has established me is better, so if only you help me with strenghth (of men), I will make a fortified barrier between you and them: bring me blocks of iron. At length, when he had filled up the space between the two mountain sides, he said, blow. Till, when he had made it (as) Fire, he said: bring me molten brass to pour over it. So they were not able to scale it, nor could they make a hole in it." But the devils were not to remain there forever.

Sura 18:98, tells us that Allah's promise will come to pass and he (Allah) will crumble it (the wall) and allow the devils to room the earth freely to cause trouble. Sura 21:96 says, that the devils will be let loose, and sally forth from every elevated place. The crumbing of the wall which withheld the Caucasians for a time is thus explained by the Qur'an it self, as the letting loose of Gog and Magog. Just as the building of the wall indicated the confinement of the Europeans to their own territorial bounds, the crumbling of the wall means that they will at some future time be let loose and they will then dominate the whole world. And that is exactly what we are experience today, the domination of the European nations over the whole word, and no one can stop them but Allah himself. The domination of the European nations is spoken of in the Hadith (sources outside the Qur'an) in various ways.

According to one Hadith "no one will have power to fight against them" (ms.52.20) According to another, "They will drink the water of the whole world." (Ku. Vol. 7, p. 2557) According to a third, God said: "I have created some of my servants whom no one can destroy but myself." in the Qur'an Sura 74:11-17, Allah says, "Leave me alone with him whom I created, and gave him vast riches, and sons dwelling in his presence, and made matters easy for him, and yet he desires that I should give more! By no means! Surely he is inimical to our messages. I will make a distressing punishment overtake him."

Historically speaking these verses can refer to Walid ibn Mughīrah and others of that time. But these verses are a general description of the European nations of the future as well; the times in which we are living in right now. I hope by reading this body of knowledge, you the reader has gained a better understanding of the devil and the times in which we are living in. Its important that we know the reality of the devil and God, as with out the knowledge to distinguish how will you know who you are following?

Salâm

SUPERIORITY

We just learned in the previous chapter that the black man, as taught by the Holy Qur'an, is the original man. Sura 2:31, tells us that the original man (Adam) was taught the knowledge of all things. Showing that the original man had supreme knowledge making him supreme over all others, even the angels themselves (the controlling powers of the forces of nature). That's why Allah asked Iblīs in Sura 38:75, "What prevented thee from submitting to him whom I created with both my hands?" The phrase "both my hands" is an idiomatic expression taken from the Arabic word "Yadiya", which means; power and superiority.

In Arabic it reads, "Mā Mana'a-Ka an Tasjuda Li-Ma Kalag-tu bi-Yadaiy".

Word for Word Translation: What prevented thee from submitting to him whom I created with power and superiority.

The only reason I am writing this is because I am tired of people accusing Elijah Muhammad of teaching racial superiority. Elijah Muhammad, taught superiority based on Qur'anic teachings no different from how the Holy Prophet Muhammad taught it. Elijah taught that the original man's knowledge is what made him supreme not his color. And when the original man lost knowledge of self, he lost his position of superiority.

Abu Hurairah said the Messenger of Allah (PBUH) said; "People are mines like mines of gold and silver; the more excellent of them in the day of ignorance are the more excellent of them in Islam when they attain knowledge." (M-Msh. 2:1).

The superiority of race over race and family over family is recognized - people are mines like mines of gold and silver - among Muslims as well as non-Muslims, but it is added that this superiority is maintained through attainment of knowledge. If persons belonging to a superior race discard knowledge, they lose their superiority. Racial or family superiority is thus subject to the acquisition of knowledge.

Sura 49:13 says, "O mankind, surely we have created you from a male and a female, and made you tribes and families that you may know each other. Surely the noblest of you with Allah is the most dutiful of you." Superiority of one race over another does not depend on nationality, wealth, or rank, but on the careful observance of knowledge, duty, and moral greatness.

"Allah will exalt those of you who believe and those who are given knowledge to high degrees." (Holy Qur'an 58:11)

Salām

References

Abdul Mannân 'Omar. *Dictionary of the Holy Qur'an (Arabic-English)*

Elijah Muhammad. *Message to the Blackman*

Dorset E. Baber. *Webster's New Universal Unabridged Dictionary – English Dictionary*

William Lane. *Arabic – English Lexicon*

Farrakhan Muhammad. *Study Guide 19*

Ismā'il ibn 'Umar (ibn Kathīr). *Tafsīr (Commentary)*

John Penrice. *A Dictionary and Glossary of the Qur'an.*

Maulana Muhammad Ali. *A manual of Hadith*

Maulana Muhammad Ali. *The Holy Qur'an, English Translation and Commentary.*

W. Wright (Grammarian). *Arabic Grammar.*

The New Webster Encyclopedia Dictionary of the English Language.

Authorities

(B) Bukhārī

(KU) Kanaz al-'ummāl fi Sunani-l-Aqwāl Wa-l-Af'āl, by Al-Shaikh 'Alī al-Muttagī.

(MMA) Maulana Muhammad Ali

(M-MSH) Muslim Mishkat Abu-lHusain ibn Al-Hajjāj

(MS) Sahīh Muslim by Imām Abu-l-Husain ibn Al-Hajjāj

(PBUH) Peace Be Upon Him

(RM) Rūh al-ma'ānī by Abu-l-fadl Shahāb al-Din al-sayyid

(RZ) Al-Tafsir by Imām Fakhr al-Dīn Rāzī

www.ingramcontent.com/pod-product-compliance
Lightning Source LLC
Chambersburg PA
CBHW031652040426
42453CB00006B/283